TODAY IS A GOOD DAY TO DIE

Dedicated to
Nigel Hollis
who first gave me confidence

The saying "Today is a Good Day to Die" comes from the North American Indian warrior tradition. It encapsulates their courage, their ability to 'live in the now', with death as part of life, and their readiness to die with dignity, whenever the appropriate moment comes.

"Farm as though you'll live forever;
Live as though you'll die tomorrow".
A New England saying

TODAY IS A GOOD DAY TO DIE

Lorna St. Aubyn

Gateway Books, Bath

First published in 1991
by GATEWAY BOOKS
The Hollies, Wellow,
Bath, BA2 8QJ

Distributed in the USA by
THE GREAT TRADITION
11270 Clayton Creek Road,
Lower Lake, CA 95457

Set in 10½/12½ pt Sabon by
Ann Buchan (Typesetters), Middlesex
Printed and bound by Billings of Worcester
Cover design by Paul Nelson

British Library Cataloguing in Publication Data:
St. Aubyn, Lorna, 1929–
Today is a good day to die
1. Death
I. Title
133

ISBN 0-946551-68-5

Contents

Foreword

In the West we have come to accept that we have a natural entitlement to live for about 80 years. The experience of the early death of a child or a friend can then leave us confused and angry. They have been cheated and, in our loss, we often look for someone or something to blame: The employer for conditions at work, defective genes passed down by the parents, smoking or tension. We want to identify why the normal pattern of life has been disturbed and to take whatever action is needed to reduce the chances of it happening again.

How different is the experience of the Middle East or of Asia where the faith of the majority remains that each of us dies according to God's will. How will we know whether our daily work-outs and vitamins buy us more time or are futile magical gestures against our destiny?

To begin to think about Death and the points at which it touches our lives quickly stirs us at the level of our deepest assumptions, normally left hidden in the area that we call our philosophy of life or religious faith. As you read Lorna St. Aubyn's clear, encouraging book, the ripples spread out into surprising areas.

She invites us to prepare deliberately for our death. Not simply by tidying our affairs, but also by working hard to forgive and let go of whatever needs to be completed in our relationships before we go. She shows us how we may prepare and practise for our dying through recognising the 'little deaths' that occur at the turning points in our life –

moving home, separation, divorce and retirement, for example.

There are chapters on suicide and abortion which I find among the most helpful in the book. She also considers the value of 'short lives' such as those of babies who live for a few hours and finds that they may often have been complete in their own way, the purpose fulfilled.

The success of the medical profession in prolonging life through spare parts surgery is also discussed. Here we are reminded of the difficult issues that arise where the quality of life suffers as the quantity of life is increased.

The nearest that we have to descriptions of how it feels to die come from those who have medically stopped living but have survived. Drawing on these recorded Near Death Experiences Lorna St. Aubyn sets out the common ground, the remarkably similar way in which these survivors have experienced their death, up to the point where they returned to life.

Anyone who can remember the death of a close relative or loved one will understand the great effect that a 'good death' can have on those who are left behind. From her own belief in reincarnation Lorna St. Aubyn encourages us to approach our dying as something that we have done many times, something that we know instinctively how to go about. Is not the death that we create one of our finest achievements?

Jonathan Powell

Introduction

Our modern Western approach to death is patently unsatisfactory. A tragic number of people approach death in terror
of the 'black hole' into which they imagine they will be
absorbed. Even those brought up in the Church seldom leave
the world totally certain of the 'everlasting life' and 'celestial
bliss' promised them, and the main body of our bereaved
retain a sense of despair because they are unable to believe
that they will one day be re-united with those they love.

This attitude towards death, so neatly summed up in that
dreary Victorian phrase, "Now among the hungry worms she
sleeps", has for too long enveloped us in a pall of fear,
preventing contact with the Higher Worlds. As we move into
this decade of great changes, it is vital that we reconsider in
depth the whole question of death and dying so that we may
be liberated from the psychological and spiritual constrictions
imposed on us by this fear.

While attempting this re-assessment, certain assumptions
will be made:

1. That we have lived and died many times before.
2. That physical birth is the limitor and death the liberator.
3. That our soul encapsulates the sum total of all our
   previous lives.

Let us then be bold and turn upside down our entire
thinking about death. Let the other worlds become home and
the Earth a place that we visit many many times. Let death no
longer be 'the Great Reaper', but a gateway to our next
initiation or change of consciousness.

If such assumptions seem difficult for the reader to accept, I would request of him an attitude of 'suspended disbelief' for the duration of this book, so that its discussions can be carried to their logical conclusions.

The author would like to reassure her readers that although she has used 'he' and 'man' throughout this book when referring to the collective human being, it has been done in the interests of non-clumsy English, NOT because of any intended slight towards womankind.

Chapter 1

Non-attachment – Fear of death – Past-life experiences – Soul groups

Non-attachment is one of Buddhism's most fundamental lessons. Travel lightly, it says, at all times prepared to leave the Earth. This precept does not in any way exclude love for the Earth and those we meet here; nor does it mean that we should skim over the surface of our lives, refusing to root. On the contrary, it is essential to learn as much as possible while here, and to make our love of Earth as deep and conscious as we can.

The distinction between non-attachment and detachment is then very important. This lies primarily in commitment. The detached person seeks to avoid commitment because it so often leads to responsibility and pain. The non-attached one is so dedicated to eventual re-uniting with the Godhead that his Earth lives are seen as a means towards this goal. But they must be touched into only lightly because an hysterical attachment to Earth causes a fundamental distortion of one's priorities.

The pain and separation inherent in human life are part of our Earth lessons. They are also, paradoxically, factors which help us to travel lightly. Constant reminders of the cycles of union-separation-reunion and of life-death-rebirth, they teach us not to despair, for nothing is final; everything is part of an on-going pattern. It is only when we come to believe that our present life constitutes our entire existence, that death becomes a subject too dreadful to contemplate. Presaging annihilation, it has to be both concealed and postponed until the last possible moment. Shackled by fear, we can make no step towards the Godhead.

This fear and over-attachment to Earth also leads us to the erroneous belief that death deprives us of the opportunity to continue the work we have been doing while incarnate; whereas in fact we simply do it in a different way from a different perspective. All the fundamental issues of love and forgiveness, growth and power, responsibility and integrity will continue to be explored from the Higher Worlds.

Once we feel at ease with the idea that we have known both worlds many many times, it becomes quite acceptable to think that our experience of death is already considerable. Whether those deaths were frightening or violent, peaceful or ecstatic, whether they came upon us unawares or were long and painfully awaited, they are part of our soul's learning. And the extent of their usefulness will be determined by the degree of awareness we bring to them. That this past will become more and more available to us, is one of the fascinating probabilities of the Aquarian Age. Through fears and phobias, dreams and meditational experiences our far-memories are now attempting to re-integrate past events and feelings into our present life. From a level long inaccessible, we are becoming able to draw consciously on all that experience.

As the separations between the two worlds and between the past and present begin to thin, the question of soul groups takes on greater importance. All the members of these groups, who have been together since their first visit to Earth, are never at any one moment all incarnated, the proportion here varying according to prevailing circumstances. Because the work that can be done by incarnates and discarnates differs, the balance between them will be constantly adjusted in order to maximize the work accomplished by the group. Here again greater consciousness is growing amongst soul group members. When on this planet they are meeting and recognizing each other more frequently; when on different planes, stronger communication between them is being established.

There is nothing final about death. Nor is it a limitation.

On the contrary, it is a gateway to new possibilities and expansions. Reunited with many of those to whom we are most closely linked, and assured that our separation from those on Earth is very temporary, we can continue our personal and group evolution, thus helping the evolution of all humanity.

Chapter 2

The between-life period – the Near Death Experience – Choice of our next life

The teaching given to us by Jesus about life after death should have brought us much joy and allayed many of our fears. He could have helped us make a huge step forward in our understanding. But the distortion of His word at the hands of the Church has instead spread confusion and fear. It is, for instance, rare that a Christian funeral be a hopeful occasion.

But now we are being given two additional sources from which to explore these questions: the communcations received through mediums, and the anecdotal evidence of those who have returned to life after being declared clinically dead, (the Near Death Experience or NDE). From information they provide, a vivid picture is forming both of the moment of death and of the conditions prevailing between lives.

This emerging literature can be of immense value, assuring us as it does that our over-all soul development is on-going and purposeful, and that on this journey we will be accompanied by our closest companions. Knowing these reassuring facts, our energy need no longer be sapped by anxiety.

Because we take into the after-life what we are expecting, ignorance and illusion are even more dangerous enemies than we may at first realize. Whether we have imagined ourselves in a place of bliss, complete with angelic choir, or in a horrific Bosch inferno, that is where we will find ourselves until such time as illusion can be unwound from us, and we can move into more appropriate surroundings. To these we will eventually be drawn through the spiritual law of Attraction which works equally effectively in both worlds, and which ensures that we are where we belong, in the company of those we need and who need us. Another great spiritual law, that of Economy, will also be at work here. Optimum learning conditions will prevail so that we advance as much as possible between lives.

From information received through both mediums and near-deathers, there would appear to be four stages through which we pass after death, except in cases such as those just described, when additional time is spent in unsuitable sur- roundings.

The first stage seems common to everyone: as the person emerges into the Light, he perceives whatever image he associates with high spiritual forces. Knowing himself entirely safe and loved, all the pain and anxiety of his dying are swept away. As he gradually becomes aware of those who are waiting for him, his joy at finding himself amongst his dearest companions is overwhelming. This first encounter always occurs in surroundings familiar to the newcomer; the unfa- miliar conditions which prevail in the other worlds would at this stage be too bewildering.

Having been made welcome, he then moves on to the second stage. In a place of healing, where all the traumas connected with his death can gradually be shed, he prepares himself to assess his recent life with the assistance of those he most trusts: the guides and helpers who have been watching over him during his recent incarnation. Whether or not he was aware of them while on Earth, he now recognizes them for what they are. An objective and non-judgmental review of his latest incarnation and his entire soul's evolution now takes place. The facts simply ARE. Acceptance of them is inevitable. There is no space for reproaches or condemnation, regrets or guilt.

The third stage of this journey is concerned with healing and learning. Some rest is always included in this time, for Earth life even at its happiest, is difficult, and it may require considerable love and care in order to restore the soul to a

1. *In all cultures those who almost die often return to report going down a dark tunnel and emerging into a radiant and welcoming light.* (Prevention, July 1973).

state where it can benefit from the learning it will now be offered. The degree of choice accorded to him at this point depends largely on his state of evolution. But whatever that state, his free will is as stringently respected in the Higher Worlds as on Earth, so that it is possible that he now refuse any further learning and simply consider this stage as a period of healing and rest.

During the fourth stage, that of defining the conditions for his next life, there will again be considerable variation in the amount of choice he is allowed. But in all cases he will receive his guides' advice for creating the best opportunities to strengthen his weaknesses and right former wrongs. And even if he is not yet advanced enough to furnish any input into his life himself, it will *never* include any circumstances to which he has not agreed. It is because of this, that esoteric teaching can state categorically that no one is ever expected to do or to endure more than he is capable of. Cases where a sense of inadequacy has led to suicide raise questions which will be discussed in a separate chapter.

During this fourth stage, longer reunions with loved ones, especially members of the same soul group, also take place. The life-experience of these soul group members is also at this point shared in one of the most beautiful examples of the law of Economy at work. The mechanics of this sharing can perhaps best be described through the image of an octopus, whose body is seen as the soul group and its tentacles as the members of the group. Each time the octopus sends one of its tentacles into incarnation, the acquired experience returns to the octopus' body and becomes available to all its other tentacles. A minimum number of incarnations are thus needed for maximum learning.

The question of how much time elapses between incarnations is one on which the various esoteric schools disagree, but it would seem logical to suppose that different periods of time are needed, depending on both the demands of the previous incarnation and the state of that particular soul's evolution.

A group of people for whom additional time between

incarnations may be needed are those who are totally unprepared for death. They may even have to return to Earth unaware that they are dead. This phenomenon of being stuck in time is usually the result of a violent or sudden death of a young person in whom the life force is still very strong. During the war this was quite frequently observed. Sir Victor Goddard, at that time an Air Vice-Marshall, came home one evening to find the 'ghosts' of two young pilots playing his piano. It took all his considerable knowledge of occult matters to convince them that they were dead, and to get them to depart definitively. It is this same phenomenon which explains certain ghosts who are seen always at the same place, going about their daily tasks, oblivious of the fact that they are no longer part of Earth life.

Delay in adjusting to the Higher Worlds also occurs when a dead person continues to be drawn back to Earth by some overpowering emotion such as envy, revenge, love, or the desperate need to complete a task. There he will cause himself great distress by attempting to accomplish what no discarnate can do.

Chapter 3

Fear of Death – AIDS – NDE

To dispel mankind's fear of death is urgent. It is stultifying the entire planet. We *must* once again, as we have done in the past, know ourselves as immortal, with nothing to fear from death. We must start working with the cycles of incarnation and discarnation so consciously that we reduce death to its proper size – simply a gateway to the next stage.

The first step towards this is to assure ourselves at a deep level that we have already died many many times. No fear of the unknown can then be connected with death. If we are merely repeating a familiar process, our energy can be spent doing it really well. Those minor deaths such as partings, divorce, moving house and changing jobs can be constructively used as practice for the ending of a lifetime.

This is in direct contrast to the attitude so frequently adopted in our society: that of sweeping death under the carpet, trying to relegate it to a position so remote that it needs no serious consideration until forced upon our notice.

Erecting such a barrier of blindness between ourselves and death has created many problems, one of the gravest being our attitude towards Nature. Although watching it visibly dying all around us, we continue to claim that science is so ingenious that a solution to the world's ecological ills will certainly be found; substitutes will be invented for those natural resources we have so greedily consumed. But the irreversibility of what we have done to our planet is gradually making this arrogant assumption ludicrous. With 50% of the wells in Poland and Hungary so polluted that they can never again be used, and all of Holland's farmland deathly sick from the effect of chemicals, this myth becomes difficult to maintain.

In the medical world a certain disarray is also noticeable. There are still, despite all our wonder drugs, illnesses such as AIDS against which we are helpless. And if such a weakening of our immune system can be occurring, what other imbalances will our polluted world create for us?

The allowing of change into our lives is a good way to start facing up to death. We are given opportunities for this in the form of illnesses, losses, moves and the deaths of those we love. If we can learn not to resist change, which leaves us in some ways poorer, but in others richer, it becomes less frightening and can be a better teacher. Through it we can look at things anew, less possessively and rigidly. By learning the lesson of non-attachment we will recognize value in everything; unfrightened by loss of the familiar, we will learn to trust that what comes next will be right for us. No better preparation for death could be devised.

This attitude is personified by those who have had an NDE (Near Death Experience). The dramatic change to which they were forcibly subjected seems to reshuffle the components of their lives so basically that no change, including death, any longer dismays them.

Until very recently near-deathers were too shy to admit to their experience, afraid that they would be thought mad. They suspected that the doctors would define their cases as hallucinations caused by oxygen deprivation. They had heard their nurses treat them as nightmared children, whose tales of other worlds could be dismissed as dreams or the consequences of anaesthesia. All would be well, they had been assured; all would be forgotten.

But they did not want to forget the slightest detail of their NDE; it was, as many of them have testified, the most beautiful moment of their lives. And now, since the floodgates have been opened by Dr Kenneth Ring's research at the University of Connecticut, their voices are being heard, telling us that millions rather than thousands of people have gone

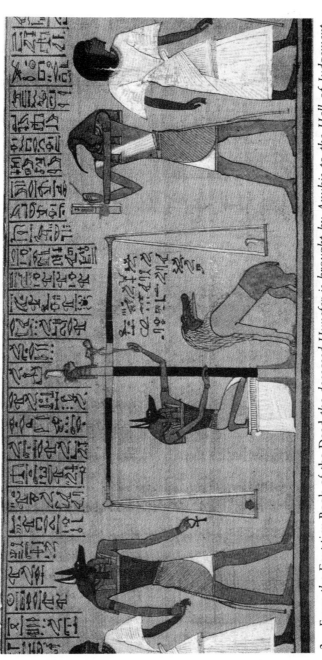

2. From the Egyptian Book of the Dead the deceased Humefer is brought by Anubis to the Hall of Judgement. His heart is to be weighed against the feather of Truth of the goddess Maat.

through this initiation, convincing them that death is no more than a transition into a new consciousness.

Whatever their nationality and background, religion and education, a fundamental common story has emerged. At the moment of physical death they instantly lost all sense of pain, and as they were irresistibly drawn through a tunnel towards a beautiful light, they heard a voice asking them whether they were yet truly ready to die. There could be, the voice suggested, something incomplete in their life. If this were so, and they felt it should be dealt with, they still had the choice of re-entering their physical body. It was unanimously reported that returning to Earth seemed a very unattractive prospect, immensely heavy and distressing compared to the beauty and peace of travelling towards the Light. Nearly everyone had been aware that their decision had to be taken before reaching a certain point in the tunnel. For none of them was the choice easy. As they progressed, their sense of joy and home-coming intensified. Only the most pressing sense of family or spiritual duty could make them choose for Earth. Even as they re-entered their body, some of them regretted their decision. All agreed that their fear of death had been conclusively dispelled. However painful our actual dying may be, and however distressing the separation from loved ones, death itself is infinitely beautiful, they all reported.

In some marvellous way these near-deathers have allowed themselves to be used as messengers from God, bringing us the glad news we have so long forgotten, that death is our friend and the other worlds are home. At no time in our history has this message been so needed.

Chapter 4

Our death as the Summing-up of our Life – Our State of Mind at Death

To see our death as the summation of our life may seem bizarre in a society where death is traditionally relegated to a dark cupboard until the last moment. Yet dying needs as much consciousness as living. If dignity, order and self-responsibility have been our code of life, we will want to die by that same code.

In order to accomplish this successfully, two things are essential: the first is to accept into our life as early as possible the cycles of death and rebirth, so that by the time we die they have become our friends and teachers. The second is to listen gracefully to any warning we may receive of our impending death, rather than denying it access to our consciousness. These warnings can prove very helpful, giving us time to put in order matters that might otherwise have escaped our attention or been postponed. A life-threatening illness, for instance, rather than being seen as an enemy could become the means whereby we focus on what still needs to be done in this incarnation. To hide such an illness from someone could be to rob him of very valuable choices for the final period of his life.

It is an extraordinary fact that although society readily accepts that women should be helped to prepare themselves, both physically and emotionally, for giving birth to a child, dying is something through which modern Westerners have been expected to muddle as best they can. Our fear of death has made preparations seem threatening rather than desirable. This situation is, however, definitely beginning to improve with the growth of the hospice movement and cancer support groups, and the increasing availability of counsellors specially trained in matters of death and dying.

Another very creative preparation for death is through the use of rituals, which can help us move successfully from one cycle to another. Although expressed in many different forms, these rituals all stem from the basic idea that with the conclusion of an old cycle, everything inappropriate to the new one should be deliberately released, so that no straggling residues remain. Regrets and nostalgia spoil all possible enjoyment of new pleasures and opportunities.

The same is true of our dying. If we are then still preoccupied with the past, we cannot fully live our immediate task: that of moving towards the beauty of the Christ light awaiting us.

The state of mind in which we die is crucial not only to the rounding off of our present incarnation, but also to the tone we set for one or more future lives. If the last breath we draw is filled with hatred and resentment, those emotions will be carried forward, and although much work on them can of course be done between incarnations, many negative thought forms can only be worked out during an Earth life.

It is of course also possible for a person to become so addicted to his feelings of violence and hatred that he cannot function without the 'buzz' of anger and indignation they give him, so he will refuse to change between lives. Even though healing is offered to us while discarnate, we have the same right to refuse it then as we have on Earth. All work on his hatred and resentment will then have to be done in incarnation.

Conversely, a profound change of heart, even in the last moments before death, can change our karma from being wearily retributive to being joyfully creative.

It follows from this that forgiveness must be one of the most important issues in both living and dying. Whether we have wronged someone or been wronged, it is in everyone's interest that our slate be as clear as possible before we go, so that we needn't yet again experience the same pain and remorse through the same people in different guises.

The growing annals of past life recalls show with painful clarity how strongly these violent emotions carry over from one incarnation to another, often poisoning them until a memory re-surges to change, in the twinkling of an eye, the deepest psychological patterning. It was the memory of being guillotined in the French Revolution which allowed, for instance, one man to begin making order of his life which had until then been constantly wrecked by an apparently unfounded seething resentment and sense of having been cheated.

In another recall, a woman saw herself in the 19th century, dying of tuberculosis. It was because of her erstwhile feeling of merciless jealousy towards her sister, who had long been the object of her husband's love, that she had now returned to Earth so dogged by her jealous nature that all men instinctively shied away from her. Having glimpsed the source of her destructive emotions, she was able to work on them in therapy and completely alter her life.

Another vital aspect of our dying thoughts concerns our feelings towards ourself. Most of us are so self-demanding. We so easily blame ourselves for what we have done and not done. Here again forgiveness is of the utmost importance. If we die in a state of self-hatred and self-recrimination, we cannot fail to reincarnate with so little self-worth that we severely restrict ourselves.

Our requests for forgiveness need not be limited to those who are geographically accessible or even still alive; neither time nor space exist in these matters. In the ritual given in the appendix of this book, it will be seen that if the person in question senses our true humility and need, his Higher Self can respond to our request.

As this two-way forgiveness takes place, an increased non-attachment will automatically follow. If this is experienced by those who love us as a disturbing withdrawal, we must try to help them understand that it is not from our love but from our Earth-ties that we are withdrawing. As these become increasingly inappropriate, we move into the next stage of our journey. By now all matters of external responsibility should have been addressed; our role is no longer to act *in* the world. Our remaining time is needed for the major transition.

The better this can be understood by friends and family, the better they will be able to help us release. Being clung to, however lovingly, can only impede our passage. Love strangles as effectively as it nourishes.

In addition to the emotional ordering already discussed, the tidying of one's possessions is another very helpful step towards non-attachment. Constant pruning also saves someone much of the trauma connected with going through the belongings of a loved one. The same is true for the ordering of one's papers which can at the same time be a very healing process for oneself. Meticulous order in business matters and a properly drawn will – preferably made with the knowledge and accord of one's successors – are also very helpful factors.

As many of us do not see the hour of our death approaching and are taken unawares by sudden illness or accident, the non-attachment described above could usefully be practised as a way of life. By not allowing sticky fingers to grasp at either people or possessions, we can enjoy them a hundred times more; travelling lightly, we will be ready to go at any time.

Chapter 5

Quality not Quantity of Life – Organ Transplants – Euthanasia

Because our contemporary world is so accustomed to making judgments from a material point of view, it is almost automatically assumed that the length of a life is all-important in determining its efficacy. We see this attitude very clearly demonstrated in our increasingly frantic efforts to prolong life at all cost through organ transplants and life-support machines. It is also more subtly evident in our reaction to the death of a baby or child. However devastating the grief involved, that death is *not* a truncation; that life is not something which 'should' have lasted longer. The soul of that infant can have fulfilled its intended purpose in 24 hours as successfully as someone who reaches three score years and ten.

To accept the rightness of a child's lifespan and know that its time here was necessary for its soul evolution, frees us from much bitterness, so that once the weight of grief has lifted, we can begin to understand the significance of the death, not only for the child itself, but also for those whose life it affected.

The possible reasons for choosing such a short earth life are numerous. The child may have needed to experience a happy welcome in contrast to a former rejection. It may have agreed to be, through the sorrow caused by its death, the catalyst for an important heart initiation. It could, alternatively, be helping to redeem – not as a punishment but as a just balancing – the cruelty in a former life of one of its present parents. The effect of the child's death on its grandparents and other close family members would almost certainly also form part of the overall picture. The spiritual law of Economy seeks always to achieve the maximum results with as few events as possible.

If we can realize that we are seeing from our Earth perspective only a minute portion of what constitutes a soul's full history, this death, however poignant and hard to bear, can hopefully one day be seen as a just and necessary part of a total cohesive pattern. Our initial rebellion against a seemingly senseless event will then be eased.

In our resentment over the death of someone young, we feel them to have been wrenched from the Earth, instead of having had time to reach maturity and then gradually drift away. We feel cheated on their behalf. In this it is almost as though we were unconsciously likening them to a tree whose life span is predictable unless cut short by lightning, disease or a chainsaw. But, unlike a tree, man has no 'natural' life span. Each of us chooses it for each incarnation. Our moment of death therefore must be the right one. There can be no question of being 'cheated'. The idea of a 'reasonable' life-expectancy as defined by insurance statistics, and constantly extended by modern medicine, falsifies our whole understanding of death and causes us unnecessary pain.

This idea that we choose our own moment of death is very clearly dealt with in Tibetan teaching. After we have breathed the precise number of breaths allocated to our incarnation, we will, they say, die. To interfere with this design would be for them an unthinkable sacrilege.

Westerners would almost unanimously oppose such a view, deeming it fatalistic and therefore retrograde. Scientific thinking has gradually convinced us that it is not only permissible but desirable that we 'conquer' nature. From this standpoint there is only a short step into the whole tricky area of organ transplants.

At first glance the arguments given to justify these are very convincing, even to those with a predominantly spiritual perspective. If a body, which is the vehicle for a spiritual entity, needs more time in which to finish its earthly task, should not its life be prolonged, they ask? But the question, when more deeply researched, becomes increasingly complex, mostly because transplant research has so far focussed its attention almost exclusively on the physical aspects of the matter. Viewing man as a mere composite of his parts, the scientists quite naturally seek to replace worn-out sections of the body in much the same way as a garage mechanic replaces a defective clutch or gear box. But here lies the fundamental misconception. We are not an agglomerate of limbs and organs. We are a *whole being* of which every part must be functioning in harmony with the rest. It is in accepting the full implications of this fact that we will understand the need to question the basic principle of transplants.

The phenomenon of rejection, which so often occurs after a transplant operation, may well contain the clue to the problem. Can it be seen as the physical manifestation by which we are being told that transplants do not in fact work in the interests of those for whom they were designed? The very high rate of rejection, especially where major organs are involved, seems to be a statement made through the physical body that this is not the correct answer to the deterioration of organs. The problem seems to go far beyond a question of techniques that could ultimately be conquered by science.

This is, of course, profoundly difficult for the scientists to acknowledge. So passionately involved in their research do they become that the end result of their work loses reality for them. The patients receiving the transplants become components of the experiment rather than individuals being healed.

And we, the public, obsessed by fear of death, have gone along with them, allowing them to persuade us that it is only a question of time before all transplants can become a safe and morally acceptable part of life.

But is this really so? Certain facts seem to militate against it. And these, with their spiritual and ethical implications, should be clearly stated. Already a totally unacceptable traffic in organs has led to legal prosecutions in several countries. The untold horrors perpetrated by the Nazis as 'scientific

3.   In the American Indian tradition, the dead warriors are shown in flight on magnificant horses in their otherworld. Overhead, an eagle flies between the Land of the Sunset and the heavenly realms.

experiments' are a hideous warning of what can happen if experimentation goes unsupervised. In the more distant past, genetic engineering, an inevitable corollary of organ transplants, is said to have been one of the major factors in bringing about the destruction of Atlantis. With robot slaves working for scientists who were unguided by any ethical standards, their civil war escalated into the use of such destructive forces that tidal waves and earthquakes finally annihilated that great civilization.

Most of us when thinking of modern advances in transplant surgery, imagine the work being done in safe controlled conditions for the benefit of mankind. But this is not necessarily the case. This is a free-for-all situation in which the discoveries could be used to further *any* ends. We are considering an area where man is acting as co-creator with God but has none of the spiritual motivation which would make this permissible.

The basic question we must ask ourselves here is whether we can rightfully attempt to protract our lives? What are the parameters within which we are working? Will we go to the extreme polarity of people like Jehovah's Witnesses who forbid all operations and the introduction of any foreign substance into the body, even blood transfusions? Or are we advocating the other extreme represented by those who have been frozen at death in the hope that scientific advances will one day allow them to live again?

Somewhere between these two views must lie the answer. In order to find it, perhaps we should start by defining our relationship to our body. If seen as the temple of our soul, a temporary vehicle necessary for our functioning on planet Earth, we must look after it. We must eat properly, sleep sufficiently, exercise sensibly, and attend to any injuries it sustains. By disregarding this, the asceticism and self-mortification encouraged by sections of the Christian Church were as off-beam as contemporary body worshippers following the precepts of Hollywood.

The idea that our body is a *temporary* gift needed for only one lifetime may help to bring us a better sense of proportion.

If we have already inhabited numerous other bodies and will have many different ones in the future, it is easier to identify less closely with our current one. It can become a friend with whom we are really in tune and whose needs we understand, rather than a creature whose death will occasion our extinction.

Even before such deep partnership has been established between soul and body, a rule-of-thumb could forbid fear and expediency dictating our actions. This would apply not only to emergency situations such as organ transplants or chemotherapy, but also to drugs which by suppressing symptoms produce temporary relief but leave the basic condition untouched.

In taking responsibility for our own bodies, we must try again and again to establish better communication with our therapist or doctor so that we can make choices. The excessive and repeated use of antibiotics is a good example. Prescribing them to save someone's life from pneumonia is one thing; using them for every minor cold or toothache is lunacy. Not only is the patient building up such resistance to them that they become ineffective when most needed, he is also seriously endangering his immune system, leaving him susceptible to such illnesses as candida albicans, a distressing condition causing digestive disorders, or ME (myalgic encephalitis), where intense fatigue, great muscular pain, depression and disorientation can incapacitate the patient for many months, even years. AIDS is also a disease closely connected with the deterioration of the immune system.

The decision to accept either a blood transfusion, a bone or skin graft, takes us a step further in allowing science to repair accidental or inherited damage. In these operations, living matter from one human being is used for the care of another. In nearly all cases – provided the blood, bone or skin has been properly 'matched' – the patient so quickly assimilates the alien matter that it soon becomes impossible to distinguish the foreign from the native. Here we still appear to remain within the realm of the acceptable, as no essential change has been wrought, especially when the bone or skin for the graft has been taken from the patient himself. The doctor's skills have merely set in motion a self-healing process.

It is with the transplanting of a major organ that some invisible but very real barrier seems to be crossed. The patient has been invaded, his life-span tampered with. And is this justifiable? If our heart, kidney or liver has reached its term, is that not a pretty clear indication that we have finished this particular visit to Earth? Do we really want, for the sake of a few more years, to introduce into our bodies a stranger's vital organ on which his every thought and action have been imprinted and will in a sense become ours? It is, incidentally, reported with increasing frequency that receivers of organ transplants are often disturbed both in sleep and awake by scenes or feelings from the donor's life. Such an amalgam of consciousness surely cannot be healthy or desirable.

One of the great difficulties here is that transplant surgery presupposes that we are dealing with a purely physical happening, or at best one that includes man's emotional nature. But the six subtle bodies are as important as the physical one and must all be functioning in harmony with the new organ. If no account is taken of our etheric, astral, mental, higher mental, and spiritual bodies, grave difficulties way beyond the obvious physical ones will follow.

These issues, which take this whole question into a different realm, need airing because although transplants are ostensibly widely accepted, if the full facts were known, public opinion might well decide that we have gone too far, and that major organ transplants, like hydrogen bombs, chemical weapons and certain other scientific discoveries are too dangerous for mankind to use.

One of these considerations is what actually happens to the patient's subtle bodies at the moment of, for instance, a kidney transplant. When the defective organ is removed, the person's etheric kidney, (as much a reality as the physical one,) still remains in place. Recognizing the operation as life-threatening, it tries to compensate for the loss in much the same way as if that kidney had become diseased. As the blueprint of the physical organ, bearing its DNA, the etheric has the built-in knowledge to do this. It is the same process of regeneration we see at work in a lizard when it loses its tail. Knowing the pattern of the new tail required, its etheric body grows a new one. The fact that our etheric organs know themselves capable of this, brings about a real conflict between them and any alien organ imposed from outside.

The operation then not only abruptly curtails the compensatory work of the etheric kidney in which it has been engaged ever since the onset of disease, but it also forces it to expend all its energy on trying to resolve the conflict between itself and the new kidney – an exhausting process which only negatively helps the patient. To treat this 'rejection' with massive doses of chemicals is not the solution.

The exact degree of interaction which take place between the patient and the donor in a transplant operation is not yet entirely clear, but it is certain that far more than a physical organ is included with this gift of life. Although difficult to prove, there are so many stories told about the personality changes which have taken place following these operations, that one cannot dismiss them out of hand. The alleged changes range from a new uncharacteristic irritability to a complete reversal of spiritual outlook. Even marriage break-ups due to altered personalities have been reported.

This whole question must also be considered from the donor's point of view. Here too the situation is fraught with dangers and undesirable features, mainly because of the process which takes place during the three days after death, when an essence is distilled from the person's physical and subtle bodies. This substance is essential to the soul's next incarnation. If someone's body is deprived of an organ at the moment of death, that essence cannot be properly formed. The donor must then await the death of the person who has received his organ before being able to move into the Higher Worlds. This means that there is not only a very disturbing link between the two people during the recipient's lifetime, but also that the donor is condemned for that period to a form of limbo. If this gives rise to an understandable resentment at being penalized for what he had imagined to be an act of charity, this too cannot be healthy for either party.

This same disregard for the existence of the subtle bodies also causes considerable damage to someone who receives excessive chemical or radiation treatment; such violence is sometimes perpetrated on their subtle bodies that much of their self-healing resources are also destroyed.

This question of medical treatment carried to excess highlights one of the most fundamental issues about life and death. When the quality of someone's life has become intolerable, should its preservation be one's only consideration? Is the use of life-support machines justified, or should people in a 'vegetable' state be allowed to retire with dignity?

In the same way that there is a clear line of demarcation between blood transfusions and organ transplants, so is there one separating the use of life-support machines for either brief or indefinite periods. When this equipment provides someone with a chance to rally his own healing powers and eventually resume a normal life, this is a wonderful use of modern technology. But if it is being utilized to maintain 'alive' someone who will never again act as a responsible human being, is it not time to allow that patient to move on to where he can resume his growth process. Consciously disconnecting the machine would then be a positive service performed.

When fear of death takes over, our judgment becomes distorted. Forgetting the sacredness of life, we no longer work with its natural cycles. And our dying is in consequence impoverished.

It is largely because of the remarkable lengths to which contemporary medicine goes in order to keep people alive — even against their will — that euthanasia is such a burning topic at the moment.

A referendum soon to be taken in Holland may make that country the first to legalize this practice. While as yet unaffected by pain and the proximity of death, people should, they argue, be given the option of dying rather than suffering untold pain. For them, the benefits of a conscious, dignified death outweigh other considerations. They even go so far as to say that if the person hasn't expressed a wish on the subject beforehand and it becomes relevant to the circumstances of his dying, some others, including a doctor, should be allowed to take the decision.

Let us first consider euthanasia from the point of view of its purest intent. In the majority of cases, the motive for precipitating either one's own death or that of someone dearly loved lies in the desire to end that life in the most harmonious manner possible. If pain has become the person's only reality and dying has been reduced to a sordid physical battle rather than a potentially beautiful event, harmony is very difficult to achieve. Respect for those who are nursing or visiting the dying person also often plays a major role in this decision, whether taken for oneself or someone else. To watch, or later remember, a loved one in a state of acute suffering is very unhelpful.

Euthanasia is both a means whereby we could take greater responsibility for our own death, and perform an act of mercy for someone else. Whatever one's view on suicide, the decision to end a 'vegetable' or pain-obsessed life, if taken with right intent, seems impossible to equate with either suicide or murder. Whether or not euthanasia conforms with the Tibetan criterion about the preordained length of our incarnation is arguable, but it would seem that in cases where modern medicine is attempting to extend that incarnation, euthanasia could allow the soul to return to its original intention.

That grave abuses could arise from legalized euthanasia is certain. In countries where medical costs are high, unscrupulous doctors and nurses could be bribed to end someone's life at great financial savings to the family. In poorer countries where medical care is scarce and hospital beds at a premium, the rapid disposal of someone with a hopeless prognosis could well occur. But it must be admitted that these practices already exist, so might it not be better for all matters relating to the old and dying to be brought under more stringent legal supervision, so that the malpractices now condoned through society's silence could be attacked? The 'cocktails' of sleeping draughts and tranquillizers with which the old are quietened and eventually killed could be banned. The safety of the elderly as unwilling organ donors could also be protected. New issues arising out of advances in technology could be openly discussed and safeguards provided. A well-written law could at the same time ensure help for those who want to die in their own time.

Chapter 6

Preparation for Death – AIDS

Because we cannot usually foresee the date of our death, preparation for it should be constant, intensifying as we grow older, and becoming the focus of our attention as the end approaches. This is not morbid or in bad taste, it is practical and desirable because it promotes a psychically healthy way of being: thoroughly of this world, but not clinging to it. To live with a sense of our own mortality intensifies our joys and softens our sorrows.

A constant vigilance over our psychological state is another important element in our preparation. Walking around heavy with hatred or resentment, anger, jealousy or fear is like living with an unexploded bomb inside us. We are forever at the mercy of destructive emotions which can erupt at the most inopportune moments; even if they do not do so, they are slowly poisoning every inch of our being.

Illusion and self-satisfaction are traps into which it is only too easy to fall. If we get into the habit of regularly and ruthlessly assessing our personality and behaviour we will be saved from complacency, that hyper-enemy of growth. This habit may also spare us an extremely painful and disorientating experience after death when all illusion is of necessity dispersed.

If death is potentially one of our greatest learning experiences, its presence in our everyday life in various forms should be welcomed rather than studiously ignored.

For those who come unprepared to their dying, hospitals and hospices are gradually providing special social workers and counsellors. Their work ranges from teaching relaxation techniques to helping release the patient's fears. Often working under most difficult conditions in the noisy, interrupted atmosphere of modern hospitals, these helpers are trained to make no assumptions about the patient, respecting his *status quo* absolutely, and though encouraging him to his limit, not pushing him beyond it. Their overall brief is to dispel as much as possible of what is standing between him and a peaceful death. The same applies to the priests, clergymen or rabbis who may more easily fill this role for some people. All of them must be free of the shyness which so often blocks discussion of death.

More hospices and small hospital units providing special conditions suitable for the dying are urgently needed. A quiet atmosphere and the on-going care for each patient by the same staff are two essential features of these places. Making the person feel really cared for and supported during this crucial period of his life is especially important now that so many people are entirely cut off from their families and roots. The loneliness level of those who die in hospitals or hospices is unbelievably high, and should be a major consideration when planning their care.

A very valuable service that can be rendered by kind, ordinary people who have a little time to spare, is that of listening to the dying. Their need to reminisce, to express their regrets and failures, their unfulfilled ambitions and distress is often very pressing. However short a time such relationships last, they can be of enormous importance.

Since the advent of AIDS the need to make sense of one's life is felt by an increasing number of young people. Although plagues and wars have in the past brought the reality of death into every age group, they have lasted for well-defined periods. AIDS, on the contrary, is spreading, so that unless we can outgrow the need for the disease, death for the young is no longer an event to be addressed at a later date. As a built-in possibility of life, AIDS cannot be accommodated as an exception, a distant threat, in the same way as have been the other diseases which primarily attack the young.

Suicide is another aspect of death particularly connected with younger people, but like drug overdosing, it is at one remove from the average person's life. For most of the young, fatal traffic accidents also remain, totally illogically, as something that happens to others. As factors influencing their attitude towards life and death, none of these has the intrusive urgency of AIDS.

Another thing which has given death reality for the post-war generation is the threat of a nuclear disaster, now in some ways superceded by fear of a world cataclysm. But in both cases these too could be kept at bay in a way that AIDS cannot. If death were to occur from either of those possibilities, it would be on such a major scale that no deep soul-searching would avail one much. If the Earth were to be rendered uninhabitable for humans, one's personal preparation for death would become a fairly academic matter.

But AIDS is forcing us to re-assess the most fundamental questions, especially, of course, those connected with our sexual behaviour. Fidelity and trust have become prominent issues. The relationship between creativity and sexuality must be reconsidered. If our sexuality is inhibited by fear of this life-threatening disease, does this dry up other aspects of our creativity? Or is that unused energy channelled into our work? A whole new dimension has also been brought to age-old problems such as prostitution. If sexual satisfaction carries the possibility of death, our old criteria about paid sex need sharp revision. And how do we deal with that deeply shocking knowledge that because of AIDS, the most creative act of which man is capable, that of producing another human being, now also carries the possibility of producing death?

Chapter 7

Suicide – Possession – Exorcism

Except for the Samaritans, that remarkable group of voluntary helpers who are available twenty-four hours a day to listen by telephone to would-be suiciders, there is in a sense no one to whom a person in danger of committing suicide can turn for an objective opinion. Anyone who goes to church knows *a priori* that everything possible will be done to dissuade him from such a course of action. Anyone working in an official capacity, such as a counsellor or social worker, would equally have to condemn his proposed suicide, as would friends or family members in whom he might confide. The latter would have an additional problem to contend with: they would be emotionally involved.

Yet all calls to courage and unselfishness from any of these groups would keep veering away from the real issue: why should he stay alive when he would prefer to be dead?

How can one answer such a question which so fundamentally puts in doubt society's very foundations? However much anyone may sympathize with the circumstances leading to thoughts of suicide, the whole thrust *must* be to try and make the person feel all right about being alive; otherwise in some subtle way their own *raison d'être* would be in question.

This basic split in our attitude towards suicide emerges most clearly when we are personally faced with someone who has attempted to kill himself. Part of us responds almost automatically to the survival instinct and attempts to restore him to life. Yet simultaneously, another part of us which respects that person's free will questions our actions. If he so

4.   *In the Zoroastrian version of the Last Judgement, the deceased
have to cross the Bridge of the Separator (Chinvat Parvatu). To the
wicked, the bridge presents a sharp edge, and they fall into the abyss
of hell. The righteous can pass over the bridge without difficulty.*

wanted to be dead, should he be denied his choice? If he has summoned the courage to go so far, should we be interfering and possibly forcing him to re-engage the whole process?

There are, of course, many cases where an attempted suicide is a cry for help rather than a desire for death. A person feels unseen and unheard. His dramatic gesture is asking us to focus on his despair. This happens particularly often with adolescents for whom the new demands and the choices, expectations and emotions can become overwhelming.

Loneliness is another major cause for this type of attempted suicide. So many people in modern society now live alone with very little back-up from that effective network of support which used to be provided by family, village, or city street life. In town, people move house so frequently that they often do not even know their close neighbours; the increase in crime keeps people at home in the evening; the well-documented symptoms of living in a high-rise apartment take their toll. Those whose jobs do not bring them into contact with other people can find themselves in conditions of insufferable loneliness.

Another category of attempted suicides which are frequently cries of pain rather than a wish to die are those of abandoned lovers. The hope that their dramatic action will bring about a reunion with their former partner is, consciously or unconsciously, an important factor here.

A seldom-recognized motive for suicide in children is their yearning to return to the other worlds, which to many of them seem far more desirable than the ugliness and pain of Earth. Still closely in contact with the perfection of life before birth, they return there by some passive means, such as allowing themselves to drift away from a seemingly innocuous disease. Knowing no fear of death themselves, they will have no idea of the pain they are imposing on those who love them.

In the eyes of the Church, suicide is a sin. We must not, they say, destroy what God has created; traditionally the punishment for taking one's own life was hell fire and an interdiction from being buried in hallowed ground. Although a less intransigent attitude now exists in most churches, the message put out over the past centuries has left a deep imprint on the collective, so that even those who consider themselves free of the Church and without fear of its sanctions, carry the underlying belief that suicide is a solution to which one should not resort. In addition to this Christian heritage, society with few exceptions exhorts us to keep trying in face of all adversity, so that seeing suicide as a failure and an opting-out, we shrink from it, both for ourselves and others.

There are however exceptions to all rules. And from whatever point of view one is speaking, it would be very lacking in compassion to condemn suicide in all circumstances. The desperate psychic fatigue, for instances, of those who have been returning to Earth for aeons, is at times experienced as almost intolerable. So much effort has already been expended so many times that they long for a respite – however brief. When a friend who belonged in this category developed pneumonia and a critically high fever, this soul-weariness became so overpowering that only a superhuman effort prevented him from gently slipping out of life.

Yet, ironically, it is those who are most powerfully prone to this deep fatigue of the spirit who would be least likely to take their own life, remembering the spiritual law which states that situations unresolved in one life must be dealt with in another. Suicide in that sense is simply a postponement of what one cannot deal with now.

Another spiritual adage states that although a man may overburden his donkey, God would never impose on anyone more than he is capable of bearing. Seen from this point of view, suicide stems from a lack of trust. The situation simply *cannot* be hopeless. As much help as needed *must* be available if only we can stop underestimating our own strength and the love others have for us. To see suicide as an error in judgment rather than a weakness helps considerably to eliminate our often judgmental attitude towards it.

Cases also exist, more frequently than one might suppose, when a person deliberately sacrifices his own life in order to set free someone he loves deeply. In order for this act of great courage to be successful, two things are necessary. First of all the psychic links between the two people must be of the closest. They would need to be members of the same soul group who had worked together in many different relationships. Only then could the death of one of them release in the other the vast amount of creative energy that had been locked into supporting the dependent one. Secondly the person taking his own life must be absolutely certain that this is the only means by which to break the pattern that made him become such a desperate drain on the other person.

In these cases of exceptional psychic closeness, such a sacrifice, consciously made, can break the most destructive patterning of many lives. Despite all the pain involved, lessons of great beauty and significance can be learned. The communication between them, unless the sacrifice is not understood or accepted, will certainly remain very strong.

Certain war or crisis situations can also be imagined where the suicide of one might save the lives of many. Surely that kind of generosity of spirit will be regarded with the greatest love.

A possibility which must be considered in connection with certain types of suicidal behaviour is whether the person is 'possessed'. Is there some malevolent entity seeking to destroy him? And if so, why? Enlisting the help of a reliable psychic to find the answers to these questions could well be the first step towards helping the person. As evidenced by many suicide notes, these entities often attack through guilt. The voices speaking in the victims' heads persuade them that the overall good will best be served by their disappearance. Exorcism by a specially trained priest or layman has saved many souls from self-imposed death.

The question of possession is a very complicated one, closely linked with the phenomenon of souls who are in limbo, not yet thoroughly dead. Some of these, still passionately attached to the world of sensation, return to Earth determined to find satisfaction through someone else's body. If their desires include a love for alcohol, cruelty, self-destruction or any form of perversion, the person into whom they have insinuated their spirit will start behaving both uncharacteristically and without any self-control.

Those who have weakened their natural psychic protection by excessive use of alcohol or drugs, or by the practice of psychic work without proper care or knowledge, are highly vulnerable to these entities. So are those prone to clinical depression: the slow movement of their chakras when in that state will facilitate an entity taking partial or full control. Hysterics and people of a mediumistic nature who have not yet learned to take charge of their skills must also be very careful of their psychic space.

These entities are of course not all destructive, but can be motivated by any of the human emotions and desires. So that it is only a small minority of them who would try to push someone to suicide. Nevertheless when attempting to help a particularly persistent would-be suicide, this possibility should be kept in mind. If a ritual of exorcism is undergone, it is vital that the person also learn suitable methods of psychic self-defence in order to prevent a recurrence of this extremely unpleasant phenomenon.

If it is a living person rather than an entity causing the damage, there are exercises which can be performed, preferably with the help of someone conversant in these matters, to cut the ties binding the two people. By ritualistically expressing his intention of re-gaining an independent status, the etheric ties linking him to the other person will be dissolved. This ritual may have to be repeated several times before the release is complete.

If the influence being exerted is strong enough to induce an attempt at suicide, you need someone very experienced to guide the session and be available if something unexpected or difficult happens. *Cutting the Ties That Bind*, by Phyllis Krystal and *Healing the Family Tree* by Dr Kenneth McCall are two books that deal with this matter in detail.

Chapter 8

Bereavement – Rescue Work

Many of our Western customs with regard to funerals, bereavement and mourning are actually detrimental to those making their transition into another world. Starting already with the deathbed, we often seem to get things back to front. Although it may seem obvious, for instance, that the most important person at that moment is the one dying – not his family and friends, this is in practice very easy to forget. The dying person's time is severely limited and if he has something he wants to say or request, he must be given the space in which to do so, rather than being swamped by the emotions of those he is leaving behind. Unlike him, they will have time enough later to deal with the event. Tears are very heavy and should be shed elsewhere. Strong emotions are also very burdensome and any deeply emotive exchanges should take place long before the final stages; if this is impossible, extreme restraint should be exercised, however passionate the feelings expressed. The dying person's mind should be allowed to concentrate entirely on his own future rather than on a shared past. This is no time for dramatic promises or demands on the part of family and friends.

Another way in which the dying person is often most inappropriately drawn back towards the world is through some variation of the words: 'I love you so much, how can you expect me to live without you.' Although intended as the ultimate declaration of love, their real effect is to make the dying person feel disloyal and guilty – however illogical this may be. To keep snatching him back, asking him to deal with our grief, is an act of great unkindness. Those who reach the higher worlds enveloped in the sadness of others, will have to deal with this before they can know the joys of being in their true home.

Amongst the many reasons for which a soul can remain partially earth-bound, the most common are exceptional love or hate which so bind it to some unresolved drama that it cannot move on. The work involved in helping release these souls is known as rescue work. It is mostly now the province of psychics, but has also traditionally been the task of certain orders of monks and nuns.

If this work is done consistently in a certain place, a thinning of the veil between the two worlds seems to occur, allowing those souls who gather there seeking help to become more easily disentangled from their earth bonds and make their final departure.

Chapter 9

Death of the Physical and Subtle Bodies

In the Tibetan tradition, great emphasis is laid on the importance of dying according to spiritual law. This period is considered, as in nearly all religions, to comprise the time of dying plus the three days following physical death. To this end, friends and family members are allowed at the death bed only one at a time, and for only a ceremonial farewell. It is a relay of priests who watch over the dying person. The immense retaining power of grief and tears is not allowed to obstruct the process of detachment which is taking place.

While the body later awaits burial in a totally isolated and silent part of the temple especially designated for these ceremonies, it is again the priests who watch over it, ensuring that when the soul is finally released, no untoward sounds or emotions will clutch at it. During those three very sacred days an elaborate ritual, in which the use of sound is important, takes place. The vibrations created by the priests' chanting and their special musical instruments facilitate the safe detachment and then disintegration of the subtle bodies to become once again pure energy. Only matter remains to be buried or cremated.

The stringent discipline described above contrasts diametrically with the tradition epitomized by a Sicilian death. There, as in many Mediterranean countries, the more dramatic the crescendo of noise and emotion surrounding a death-bed and funeral, the more is everyone satisfied; the more violent the feelings displayed, the more convincing is one's love thought to be. But presumably, the poor person dying is having a hard

41

time, all his attempts to veer upwards being constantly reined in by fresh outbursts of love or recrimination, bitterness or demands.

At the funeral itself it is as though the ancient goddesses take over and will be satisfied by only the most excessive behaviour. Swathed in a sea of black, they rend the country-side with the shrill sounds of grief.

But what effect is this having on the deceased? For although the process of death has now been completed, it is unwise, so the Tibetans tell us, to enmesh even the body with such violent emotion. The dead person is by now rightfully occupied with other concerns and perspectives.

The wearing of black as a sign of respect and grief, though still observed in certain countries, is a custom fast dying out in the Western world. The perpetuation of the habit of grief, which mourning clothes encourage, is constructive for neither the deceased nor the mourner; it crystalizes the situation, making progress difficult.

Another hopeful sign is the growing trend towards funerals being called a 'Celebration of a Life' (see Appendix). Instead of lamenting an ending, they are giving thanks for the deceased's stay on Earth.

5. *Birds often appear as a guide for the soul journeying between the two worlds. This gold medallion of a soul-bird is from Scythia.* (9th cent. BC).

Chapter 10

Life-threatening Illnesses

The question of whether people should know when they have a life-threatening illness is a very emotive one which needs reviewing in the light of what we have said about the fear of death being so destructive. Dangers or anxieties that are brought into the open being less sapping than those that lurk unexpressed in the background, one of the most effective ways of dispelling part of this fear is to make certain that we will be told if we have contracted a life-threatening disease. An agreement made with a trusted friend or spouse could ensure this. If, on the contrary, someone feels strongly that he would rather *not* know of such a situation, that too can be the subject of a pact.

Some of the advantages gained from knowing if we are seriously ill have been discussed earlier in relationship to preparing for death. But it must also be said that for some people, especially those without faith in an after-life, this knowledge can be devastating. To impose unnecessary fear and misery on them would be as unconstructive as depriving the others of the information they need. If no wish either way has been expressed by someone who becomes grievously ill, great care should be taken to sense his soul's need.

Another point to consider is who should break the news. At the bottom of this list lies the consultant, not because of any inherent lack of sensitivity or kindness amongst the medical profession, but because he will know his patient in only a very limited way and can have no real idea of how he will react. Also – and this is a very crucial consideration – he is in no position to provide any help that may be required as a result of his prognosis. The other danger into which consultants sometimes fall, often at the insistence of their patient, is that of making too specific a prognosis. This can effectively deprive the patient of all fighting spirit.

Ideally it would fall to the family doctor to inform the patient of his condition. Being well acquainted with him and his circumstances, he should be able to help formulate acceptable plans for present care and future contingencies. But alas . . . so few family doctors now exist, especially in large towns.

So who else is there to take on this difficult task, including that of receiving the full force of the patient's initial outburst of grief and resentment? Whoever it is, it should be someone close enough to know the practical and spiritual resources available to him.

Although meant as a kindness, excluding someone from such an important period of his life by concealing the truth about his health seems somehow insulting, a denial of his right of choice. By presupposing that death is frightening to him, we accord him no space for growth; we severely impoverish his death, which can be a great transformer, even friend.

The acceptance that death is not a failure of life, but a natural part of life's cycles, makes it a far less daunting prospect. When we are ready to go, we can do so with as little fuss as possible, just making sure that all relationships, especially the closest, have been properly severed.

Chapter 11

Life Review – Children with Life-threatening illness

A person's very natural need to review and discuss his life as he approaches death can be very painful to his close family and friends, especially if the issues surfacing are ones that should have been resolved years ago, when their resolution would have avoided much pain. However difficult the listener may find this, he should not interfere with the person's anguish, but allow him to clear as far as he can those matters arising from the past.

Forgiveness will certainly be an important issue at this point. He should be helped in any way possible to forgive and be forgiven, whether the people involved can be present or not, and remembering that there is no divide between the two worlds: the giving or receiving of forgiveness can take place as freely with a discarnate as with someone still alive.

As well as needing to review their life, most people who know themselves to be mortally ill need to talk about their fears and expectations. Again, however painful this may be to the listener, he should try to help take the sharp edge of loneliness from dying. If he can help draw together the bouquet of the dying person's life – *including* the shames and sadnesses, the fears and wasted opportunities – he will have given him a very sacred present.

If at all possible, these exchanges should take place long before the final moments. But if no opportunity has arisen before, or no one has dared acknowledge the proximity of death, allowing this review even right at the end is better than nothing.

Children are in a way more able to cope with their own death than grownups. Not being so weighted down by their lives, they can slip away with a minimum of fuss. Still closely in touch with the Godhead from which they only recently travelled, they do not see their return as a hazardous journey.

They are also not yet conditioned by society's taboos. In her book on children in hospital with life-threatening illnesses, Dr Elisabeth Kubler Ross tells us that no matter how doggedly the children's families refuse to discuss the possibility of their child's death, concealing their own anguish in plans for the future, the children themselves *know* and accept the facts. Yet they also know that they can bear the truth far better than the older generation who need in some way to be protected from it. So when told during visiting hours about the red bicycle they are to receive for Christmas, they respond with polite appreciation. But as soon as their parents leave, pretence is discarded and their imminent death returns quite naturally into their conversation.

For the children, death has become so familiar through their own increasing weakness and the regular disappearance of their companions, that they feel no fear or anxiety. When needing a grownup's advice or help on death, they turn quite naturally to the nurses, knowing that because they are not personally involved, their answers will be truthful.

This need for honesty, which is as strong as the compassion shown for their parents' distress, emerges in nearly all their drawings, some of which are illustrated in Dr Kubler Ross's book. Even if partially unconscious, these pictures show the extent of their desire to declare their awareness: in nearly every one, the figure of a dead child appears.

Are these children not helping us to understand how much adults also need to be open about death despite all they have done to hide this need in a fog of fear? In the simplicity of their deaths are they not helping us to remember what so many of us have forgotten: the worlds we lived in before we were born, that time when the magical child in us was still so close, and the days when we knew of the existence of fairies? If those dreams and visions could once again make us part of all life and of God, could we not perhaps find death as uncomplicated as do the children?

Chapter 12

Hospices – Practical Preparations for Dying – Funerals

The growing hospice movement is doing a wonderful job overcoming many of the difficulties which arise when death takes place in hospital. There the main concern inevitably has to be the other patients; their susceptibilities and fears must not be aroused any more than necessary. This produces a disastrous atmosphere of concealment, almost shame, around the cubicle in which the death is taking place.

The limited visiting hours of hospital also create a problem. Although it could be very beneficial to have a relay of friends and family members constantly attending the dying person, this is often contrary to hospital regulations. And although a private room free of these restrictions is provided whenever possible, this is often available for only the last few hours.

In the hurly-burly of a ward, with constantly changing staff, the interruptions of cleaners, other people's visitors, doctors' rounds, the newspaper trolley, and the close proximity of other patients, it is difficult to die in peace with dignity. The silence considered so essential by the Tibetans is non-existent. So is privacy, of which the flimsy curtain pulled around the bed is a mockery, barely separating the person from that world he is trying to leave.

In a hospice, on the contrary, only the needs of those who are close to death have to be considered. There can be greater flexibility of visiting hours, more consistent contact between the specially-trained staff and patients. The atmosphere can be quiet.

Out of the hospice movement there has emerged a new and very helpful development in the field of special care for the dying. Teams of doctors and nurses visit private houses to help create optimum conditions for a person's last weeks or months.

Whether someone is in a hospital, hospice or at home for the final stage of his life, a great service that can be rendered by a friend is to help with any practical matters still outstanding. The disposal of special bequests is one of these, a procedure which can be very touching. When jewellery or pictures, or small objects connected with happy memories are given to family members and friends, they are a beautiful link between the two worlds. The more care that is taken to ensure that each person receives the object right for him, the more rewarding this will be.

Until lately, funerals tended to follow a set pattern. Now, more and more, the friends and relatives are planning them in great detail with beautiful results. Through their choice of music and flowers, the texts to be read and the atmosphere of the church, so much of the deceased can be evoked and so much given to those who attend the funeral.

Until quite recently, it was a normal part of the Western death process for the body to remain for three days at its home before being removed for the funeral or cremation. During this time, family and friends visited the deceased and afterwards exchanged condolences and family news. It was considered imperative that during those three days the body should never be alone. The prayers of those who watched over it were known to be of great assistance in his transition from one world to another. It is a tragedy that this tradition is fast disappearing, even amongst the Jewish community.

The custom of holding open house for three days after a death is still honoured in many cultures, and although in some ways harrowing, it is in others very desirable. During this period of enforced sociability, the self-discipline required helps contain the chaotic quality of the family's grief. They also receive much consolation from the presence of those who share their sadness. By the time the funeral is over, the first layer of anguish has been dispersed, and in most cases they are again ready to function in the everyday world.

Social conditions in the West have joined with the decline of religious influence to hasten the disappearance of these traditions. Smaller dwellings have made it more difficult to accommodate the coffin for three days. People's mobile life-style seldom gives them enough support from family and friends in the vicinity to form the needed relay of mourners. The multi-religious society now existing in so many Western countries has also been a factor here. What was normal and accepted in cultures where most people shared the same views on death, can become so confrontational in an alien country that it is virtually impossible to observe the old customs.

In addition to these practical considerations, there have also been subtle changes in our attitude towards death which have culminated in our present passion for trying to disguise its reality, both visually and through a bewildering use of euphemisms. The presence of a coffin in a high-rise block of apartments for three days could, for instance, create such adverse feeling that it would be impracticable. For the same barely-conscious reason, less and less time is now allowed to the whole process of dying and mourning. Outwardly this is attributed to modern pressures of work, but inwardly we are trying to persuade ourselves that those things to which we give little time are without great importance.

Out of these changes was born the funeral parlour. But however well run, they are not ideal places in which to spend the days of transition. The Beings of Light which accompany all deaths are of course present, but without the much-needed human contribution in the form of constant prayer, their work is incomplete. Another desirable element which is missing are the vibrations of his home that could provide a familiar and reassuring background to his gradual detachment from Earth. The agitated atmosphere of a busy funeral parlour also cannot provide the reverence and serenity which would have built up around the body in a civilization where death was a temple matter.

These changes have also contributed to the unsatisfactory

manner in which we now have to bid farewell to those whom we were unable to see prior to their death. Saying goodbye to a flower-covered coffin standing in front of a church altar gives none of that reality to his death which will later make it easier to live with. Actually seeing a friend or relative dead is nearly always very helpful.

This is particularly true for children. Although done with the best of motives, it is not a kindness to protect them from this sight. Their imaginations can provide far more frightening images than the reality of a known face that is apparently asleep. It will also reassure them about the person's whereabouts. They will associate him with the familiar surroundings in which they last see him rather than with the fires of the crematorium or the dark earth of the cemetery. Seeing someone dead can also help a child realize that the body does not constitute the real person. Like clothes shed each evening, it has been shed at the end of its life; the person's real essence has quietly moved to another dimension, a concept quite easy for most young people to accept.

For a child who has been forbidden the sight of a beloved parent or grandparent, there can be a long period of agony during which his fantasies allow him to half-believe that the person will return. Or if the deceased has been a frightening figure in the child's life, his disappearance without evidence of his death will mean that his power continues as strong and terrifying as before.

Chapter 13

Mediums – Guidance

In the forty years before and including the First War, spiritualism became a matter of intense interest to a large number of scientists who sought to fathom its many strange phenomena such as apports and ectoplasm. It also became extremely fashionable. Several prominent figures such as Sir Arthur Conan Doyle were deeply committed to it. During this period, the communcations received were of a very personal nature. Contact was seen to be established between the two worlds, but little teaching of general interest was received.

During the period between the wars, the movement was less active. Then in the Fifties the Spiritualist churches began to spread rapidly. Large meetings were held all over Europe and the United States at which messages from other planes were given to members of the audience.

Then another shift occurred. Now that proof of survival was no longer the main concern of mediums, it became possible for them to begin working on a one-to-one basis with clients who wanted guidance on specific subjects. Their ability to shift consciousness and then allow an entity to speak through them became used not only to communicate with the dead, but also to allow the mediums' guide to offer comment from a different perspective on all aspects of life on earth and beyond.

In the past few years 'channelling', as it is now called, has grown somewhat alarmingly, especially in the United States where a rash of channelled books of dubious quality are appearing. An important thing to remember is that the level of guidance that can be given by a discarnate depends entirely on the level he had reached when on Earth, so that there is as wide a difference of quality in channelling as there would be if a random group of incarnates spoke on similar subjects. Being dead accords one no special wisdom. However, where the quality of guidance is high and the integrity of the medium very clear, interesting and helpful information is being brought through.

The ability to receive guidance directly is now slowly passing into the hands of more people. Each of us has, from birth, a guide. How much we wish to contact him and make use of his teaching for ourselves or others, is entirely up to us. Telepathic communication with those to whom we are closely linked in both worlds is also now more available to us if we choose to develop our psychic abilities.

Strict spiritual laws govern communication between worlds and these should be meticulously observed. Details of these procedures are not appropriate to this book, but a few general principles could helpfully be stated.

Occult literature insists that a resting period of at least three months should be allowed before any communication with the newly-dead is attempted. This time is needed for adjustment to his new circumstances. The departed soul may send a spontaneous message during this period if he feels that someone on Earth urgently needs it, but no contact from this side should be instigated. Earth matters are for the moment not his concern; they can only hold him back. Undemanding love is the only appropriate help that can be given to stabilize the newly-dead. Those who have not very seriously contemplated death while on Earth will benefit particularly from this.

Directives as to the type of questions we may hope to have answered are also very clear; those of a trivial nature are no longer appropriate. During the years when belief in mediumship was being established, questions that established proof of the identity of the communicating entity were admissible, but now that this has been done, the dead should not be disturbed in order to provide further repetitive proof. The question must then be serious enough to warrant the communicating soul diverting his attention from his current work. Colouring your question with your own emotions and distress is something else expressly forbidden by spiritual law. This can be very painful and counterproductive for the deceased, who should not be drawn back into Earth sorrows and conflicts unless he himself choses to be.

Many people find that, even if they don't receive formal messages from someone close to them who has died, they receive silent ones. This happens especially easily if they are still living in the house they once shared. A book open at a certain page, or a song on the radio may well convey the exact message needed at the time.

Chapter 14

Bereavement

Important as it is not to slop one's grief over the dead, it is equally important that the bereaved thoroughly grieve their loss at the appropriate time and place. Nothing is more stultifying than to store unexpressed sadness. It can so fester in the heart chakra, or so freeze it, that no love can be expressed.

The cycles of reincarnation are said to include a period of bliss between lives. When we eventually carry this memory more consciously into Earth life, it will help alleviate some of our sadness at being separated from someone we love; part of us will be able to rejoice that he be temporarily spared the pain of incarnation.

The process of grieving can fortunately be postponed. If at the time of an important death we haven't the emotional strength or inner space to mourn the passing, the opportunity has not been lost. Our grief can be dealt with months or even years later. This may, strangely enough, prove to be even more cathartic than an immediate reaction, because we will no longer be in the grip of our first overwhelming misery.

A child who has lost a parent at an early age can benefit particularly from this fact. At the time of the death, his sense of being cheated may so overwhelm him that all his mourning turns inwards in a most destructive way. Trapped there, it will manifest as the needy inner child who sabotages his whole adult life. Whatever he is given or achieves brings him no satisfaction; the feeling that fate has done him an irreparable injury dominates his entire psyche. If he can re-live with a psychotherapist the death of that parent and everything connected for him with that period of his life, he may very well be able to separate the two so that by really mourning the parent rather than his own loss, a major shift can take place.

Another disastrous thing that can happen to a child whose father or mother dies, is that the surviving parent finds it impossible to talk about the death. Openly or tacitly a ban of silence is imposed. Feeling guilty to be even thinking about his missing parent, the child moves into a fantasy world which includes the parent and which often becomes far richer than the real world. Here too it is only a retrospective mourning that can put things to right.

Both these situations can also arise in cases of divorce and separation, an increasingly common trauma with which children must find some way of dealing. At times these unpatterned ruptures in family life may have an even more devastating effect than the finality of death. Mourning the lost unity of the family can be a great help.

This sense of being cheated, which for a variety of reasons obsesses so many people's lives, is one with which we do not want to die. The karmic entanglements arising out of unresolved resentments are particularly sticky. If we are not to bring a whole new stultifying set of circumstances connected with this life into our next incarnation, we *must* before dying break up the old patterns surrounding loss.

Mourning the death of a child so that its loss can become a source of love and compassion rather than an overwhelming sadness or bitterness is perhaps one of the most difficult things to achieve. Often these deaths seem to destroy the very *raison d'être* of their mother's lives, or indeed of a marriage. Quite frequently, especially if the tragedy is compounded by the fact that the mother cannot have more children, she, or possibly even both parents, lose their faith, so unfair and cruel does the death seem. When most needed, God is doubted. How can He exist, they ask, if He allows such things to happen?

But in their grief they are overlooking a most fundamental

issue: free will. It is not God who 'willed' or even 'allowed' this death. It was the child's soul that chose to remain here such a short while. Only the recognition of this fact can eventually bring peace to those involved, thereby making the child's life complete and worthwhile.

6.   *A young athlete at the moment of death, dives into the waters of Forgetfulness.* (Roman Paestum, 480BC).

Chapter 15

Dying-tidy – Violent Deaths from the Past

Both the title of this book and the New England proverb quoted at the front of it urge us to live as though we will die tomorrow. By this it is not meant that we emulate Philip II of Spain who slept in a sarcophagus so as never to forget his mortality. Nor is it proposed that we exclude life as did those widowed Victorian women who pulled down the blinds and spent the rest of their dreary lives waiting to die. We are here to be as *alive* and aware as possible. Yet, at the same time, death needs to be recognized as part of all life, an acceptable ingredient which helps us tread the Earth lightly, not over-cumbered with our mortality.

A friend of mine who loves life enormously coined the adjective 'dying-tidy' for the state in which she leaves her desk, her kitchen and her cupboards whenever she goes away for any length of time. That piece of the world for which she is personally responsible is at all times ready for her to step out of it. That is not morbid; it is sensible. As well as sparing those who will eventually take over, it helps her keep a respectful detachment from matter, which although it should not be despised or belittled, should not emprison us.

Dying-tidy is a concept that could easily be expanded for use with relationships and work. A relationship that is dying-tidy could not include unresolved issues, sulks or resentments; these would have to be processed as they arose. At work the situation would be monitored so that a sudden death would not occasion piles of unfinished business. Group work would be organized so that ego never pushed anyone to become irreplaceable.

If this way of living could become deeply engrained enough, even a violent or unexpected death could presumably be dealt with. These deaths are seldom physically painful because the etheric body is shot out of the physical one so rapidly that no pain registers. The shock, however, can be devastating. If the person is in addition completely unprepared for leaving Earth, incredulity and distress will intensify the shock. Accident victims for instance, especially young ones, can need a lot of help in passing over.

Violent deaths in former lives can be the source of grave difficulties in the present one. People who have at some time died under torture often experience paralyzing fears and nightmares which may start at a very early age. Victims of a hanging may find formidable difficulty in expressing themselves, their throat chakras having been so damaged; here only intense psychological or shamanistic work will permanently repair the harm. Those who have drowned in a former life inevitably suffer from the obvious fear of water covering their heads, but the terrifying memory may also manifest in a more subtle form, such as feeling drowned by excessive emotions, or terrified by the lack of boundaries represented by an ocean. If those violent deaths have not been properly processed and integrated during the period between lives, they can be very destructive.

We can deal with this in one of two ways. Our first option is the induction of a past life recall, a tricky business on which not to embark lightly. But if undertaken with the right motives and the help of a reliable therapist, the past violence can be so effectively released that it loses all power. By reliving that death – a potentially very traumatic experience – it becomes properly separated from the present personality, so that although it is part of our past and has therefore in part formed us, it is no longer strangling us psychically.

The chances are high that we have experienced one or more violent deaths during the course of all our Earth lives. Some or none of them may be relevant to this incarnation. If they are, remembering them will probably release some of our deepest fears and phobias.

Our second option for dealing with this is by going to a healer. Here there are two main streams from which to chose: a traditional layer-on of hands would hope to disperse the fears through channelling the healing power of love; those with psychotherapy training would try to separate the person from his fears through such ritual as 'cutting the ties'. In both instances, recall of the actual facts would probably not be necessary.

If a shamanic healer's help is sought, there are again many different traditions which should be carefully investigated before a choice is made. The healing practiced by a shaman cuts deeply to the core of a problem; it is therefore an ideal tool with which to disempower horrific earlier deaths. But it is not for the faint-hearted.

One of the most drastic methods used by shamen is that of taking a person back to the event which has traumatized him, and there changing its outcome. To do this effectively requires a great deal of skill; it also demands considerable trust on the part of the person seeking help. There are several possible variations to this ritual, but the basic scheme is as follows: the client sits in the centre of a circle which has been drawn on the ground or floor. Within that circle is safety, assured by those surrounding it. In front of the client sits the person trained as an 'anchor', someone whose energies are strong and stable and who can summon help from the Earth herself. The shaman with his drum stands outside the circle. All those present already know the full details of the death that is to be re-lived.

Let us imagine as an example, a young Indian who many years ago failed a tribal initiation. As a result, but *not* as a punishment, he was torn apart by wild animals. The memory of that pain and fear has half-haunted him through several lives; even more damaging has been the fear of once again failing. It has in fact prevented him from attempting much of which he was capable in this lifetime. By returning to the past, accompanied by those whose whole intention is focussed with him on changing his fate, he can successfully accomplish the initiation he formerly failed.

As the shaman's drum begins to beat, the client, his eyes shut, goes back to the exact circumstances preceding his former death. He is once again that young Indian. He is in the desert at dawn. Slowly the wolves approach from all sides for their fatal attack. This is the crucial moment; if he allows terror to engulf him now as it did then, all will be lost. The drum beats more loudly. With immense courage and trust he summons the *certainty* that the power of the shaman and his clan members *can* change the events of that day. All around him he feels the tremendous instinctual power and wisdom of the animal kingdom which has been invoked; the assistance of the Earth energies called on by the 'anchor' also strengthen him. As the wolves approach, the shaman's drum beats still more powerfully. But this time he is not alone. The immense strength offered him by all his helpers joins his own strength in which he now at last believes. He *can* now defeat the wolves. He stands up. This time he does not falter. For a long moment he and the leader of the wolves stare silently at each other. Then, recognizing in the young boy that courage and self-confidence he once lacked, the wolf lies down at his feet. So do the rest of the pack. The wolves can become his teachers instead of his killers.

For a little longer the shaman's drum continues to beat steadily, holding the circle in perfect balance between earth and sky. Then it swells in volume to a wild crescendo. Then stops. The work has been accomplished.

Chapter 16

Cataclysms – Murder

Death as a result of a major cataclysm is a deeply marking event. The feeling of helplessness and panic experienced during a volcanic eruption or an earthquake, for instance, can be carried forward into many lives, especially on the emotional level. Even if the body has absorbed the memory of being burned or crushed, feelings of remorse at not having saved a beloved child, or terror that danger is ubiquitous may well be retained by subsequent personalities and be very difficult to dispel.

An interesting aspect of mass destruction is touched on in a report on the dreadful air raids sustained by Plymouth in 1942. In addition to the havoc wrought on its docks, entire streets of the town were destroyed, killing thousands of civilians. For two days the rescue teams worked without respite in appalling conditions. On the third day, although the bombing continued unabated, observers reported in different words the same feeling: at a certain level, peace had descended on the battered town. Exactly what had happened most people did not pretend to understand; they could only express a certain acceptance of what would have seemed to be a totally unacceptable situation.

But one of them, a nun who had been nursing the wounded, made a significant comment. Those who had died in the first two days of the raids, she said, had returned. They were there, helping and consoling. What is particularly interesting here is how normal spiritual law can be superceded when human need is great enough. In the ordinary course of events, those souls who had been killed should have been resting and recovering from their dreadful death. But so strong was their love and distress for their fellow citizens that they returned exceptionally to spread a cloak of peace over their town.

The violence of a murder produces quite different results from accidents or cataclysms, mainly because two lives become so closely intertwined, especially in so-called '*crimes passionels*' where phenomenally strong emotions weld together the murdered man and his killer with bonds of steel, ususally creating karmic entanglements for many lifetimes.

Other interesting questions are raised by what one might at first sight describe as haphazard murder: the apparently motiveless killing, for instance, of a young woman parked by a motorway, or the indiscriminate massacres now occurring all over the globe. These events terrify yet fascinate us, largely because their perpetrators seem to be working from a quite different set of rules and values from those we understand. How can we enter into the thinking of someone who clubs to death an old woman in her wheelchair and then leaves her house empty-handed? How can anyone be angry or desperate enough to machine gun a dozen people who play no part in his life? Is he trying to destroy his own unbearable sense of isolation? Or does he want to make himself noticed by whatever means? Or is there some other explanation that takes us into the intricate realm of karma: the law of cause and effect? Are his victims in fact closely linked to him? Would events from their past explain these seemingly nonsensical happenings?

A martyr as defined by the Oxford dictionary is someone who "undergoes the death penalty for persistence in Christian faith or obedience to law of Church or undergoes death or suffering for any great cause". So there is a variety of reasons for which one could experience one of the particularly unpleasant deaths devised by imaginative mankind. Yet martyrdom, however traumatic, is probably the violent death most easy to assimilate during the afterlife, because the martyr will have surpassed himself. Whatever his religion or cause, he has put it above his own life, and of that he can be proud. If his death under torture also saves the lives of others, he will have left Earth with a sense of completion and purpose that few achieve.

It is only if the martyred one is unable to forgive his torturer, seeing him primarily as an evil person rather than the instrument of an evil system, that future karma need arise between them. Extreme cases like these illustrate dramatically the spiritual dictum that if we can *accept* a death, however unbearable, no adverse karma will result.

Of all the deaths imposed by man upon man, those occurring in concentration camps seem the most ignoble in that they prove nothing and help no one. As the victims of racial or national persecution, rather than as individuals, their inhabitants are stripped of what is *essential* to every human being: the right for his death to be a completion rather than a truncation of his life.

When an individual is killed by another individual for idealogical reasons, we can make of his death a statement valuable to the collective, so that his killer, despite any contempt he may express for that person's beliefs, race, or political views, can acknowledge him as a creature of courage and integrity. But in the camps it is as a member of a queue that he enters the gas ovens, as a number in a line that he faces the firing squad. His life is not affirmed by such a death. Robbing a man of that sense of uniqueness which makes him know himself a beloved spark of the divine returning to the Source is a crime beyond any that we can imagine.

Chapter 17

Abortions – Miscarriages

When considering the 'deaths' that occur as a result of abortions or miscarriages, the first question to ask is when does the soul enter the body of the child? The Roman Catholic Church teaches that they are united at the moment of the foetus' quickening, i.e. at 17 weeks. This date is also used by the medical profession as the basis for saying that it is 'all right' to abort a child prior to that time. Later on the operation could prove physically unsafe for the mother.

The esoteric view of this question is somewhat different. It asserts that from the moment of conception, the soul stays very close to its parents, getting used to them, preparing them for its arrival, but that it enters its physical body only just before the moment of birth. A foetus that is aborted or miscarried has therefore not been fully claimed by its prospective soul.

The effect on a woman of losing her baby before term is often devastating. To those who have never been pregnant, their grief may even seem bewildering. "But you didn't even know the baby", they say. "How can you be so sad?" Yet most women in these circumstances mourn deeply.

The anticipation of motherhood, whether desired or not, sets off a chain of expectations that very quickly take over the woman's being, so that if the process is foiled, voluntarily or not, a very painful disentanglement has to take place. Because this fact is often not fully realized, and also because abortions are so shrouded in fear and guilt, the necessary grieving for the child is frequently not done.

The other element that is usually not dealt with satisfactorily in these cases is that of guilt. However illogical it may seem, a miscarriage is often experienced as a failure towards the unborn child. A whole series of 'If only . . .' thoughts are sparked off, most of them involving blame of herself for lack of care: Had she not been so overstressed . . . Had she not made some physical effort that was too great . . . Had she not had an abortion when she was younger . . . Had she not taken the pill for so many years . . . The list is long, and often the reproaches are so divorced from reality that it is very difficult to comfort her.

For women who have deliberately terminated their pregnancies, the situation is even worse. Logic is of no help. Even if untold difficulties would have awaited the child: severe mental or physical handicap; the absence of a father to help bring it up; great economic distress; the stigma of being illegitimate etc. etc., these practical considerations do little to dispel the guilt. If the child's father has been told about the baby, he too often experiences strong feelings of desolation at having created and then destroyed a being for whom great love could have grown.

Even where no religious considerations complicate the issue, the moral prohibition against abortion seems to be so deeply engrained, that self-blame is seldom avoided. Compounded as it is by the protective mechanism set up by nature, abortion is a drastic act from which recovery is not easy.

Certain communications received through mediums shed a new and interesting light on this whole question. Why, for instance, should a soul voluntarily undertake the painful process of descending into Earth's coarse vibrations for only long enough to be aborted? The most common answer to this seems to be that its previous life was so negative or terrifying that it can't yet face a full-length incarnation. This brief encounter with Earth is the best way for it to re-engage in its evolutionary pathway.

The other major reason why a soul might chose to be aborted is if it had some special message for the woman involved. It could, for instance, be attempting to awaken her maternal instincts, or reminding her of something from the far past of which she needs to be conscious in this life. If she had once abandoned her child, or neglected it in favour of a man, her present sorrow could help her fully appreciate the love and responsibility involved in motherhood. For the baby to have undertaken such a task almost certainly implies that the two souls involved are deeply linked.

Looking at the problem from the woman's point of view, we see that she too has accepted to learn through the emotional distress of an abortion. Why would she have agreed to this possibility? The most likely answer is that she wants to change some pattern she has followed for several lifetimes. If this has included prostitution, for instance, she might now want to experience the full pain of losing a child instead of viewing abortion as a mere occupational hazard. She might also be trying to break in herself one of the old patterns that so bedevilled the degenerated temple life of many civilizations. There women were used as manufacturers of foetuses for temple sacrifices. To those women abortion would have been a normal part of life.

Another quite different scenario involves the learning of compassion. The woman could, for instance, when in a male body, have shown utter callousness towards someone he had made pregnant. Had he, alternatively, been one of the temple priests who broke the spiritual law by using the foetuses' life force to gain personal power, particularly unpleasant karma would need redeeming. The complex possibilities here make it very understandable that so many people have been willing to include an abortion in their learning. Certainly there have been ample opportunities for using it latterly when its legalization in so many countries has dramatically multiplied its incidence, and it has at the same time become in Communist countries the only method of birth control.

However pressing the practical or medical considerations leading to an abortion, it rarely fails to leave behind very unpleasant after-effects. Whether carried out in unsavoury conditions or in the clinical harshness of a hospital, it is nearly always experienced as an assault on one's most private being.

The enacting of a ritual can be very helpful in dispersing this guilt and grief. The one given in the appendix can be adapted to any individual needs and tastes.

Where exceptional circumstances, such as rape, may have made it impossible for the woman to love her child, performing the ritual could help separate the child's death from its conception, allowing some of the horror and hatred associated with this memory to be transmuted into love.

As more and more men are wanting to share responsibility in all areas of parenting, a ritual adapted for the father of an aborted child is also included in the appendix. Although many men still adopt the old attitude that if a woman gets 'caught' she must suffer the consequences alone – payment for the operation being the best she can expect – this form of behaviour is now luckily less prevalent, partly due to society's general change of attitude towards women.

An interesting speculation with which I would like to close this chapter concerns the invisible playmates children so often claim to have. Can it be that the souls of the aborted foetuses, still partially earthbound, are attracted for a short period of time to the company of children, by whom they are not frightened as they are by the harsh world of adults? Through this gentle contact they come to appreciate a very positive, reassuring side of human life. The other intriguing observation here is that the mothers of these children have often had a miscarriage or abortion just before or after their birth. Their 'playmates' could in that case be their own siblings.

Chapter 18

The Dying of the Earth – Concentration Camp Sites

Until recently, the world was lovingly tended by her inhabitants. They knew that a deep symbiotic relationship existed between man and the Earth, and it never occurred to them to abuse her, let alone bring about her partial death. Her animals were killed for food, not sport. There was no over-cropping and impoverishing of the soil. Then gradually man stopped seeing himself as a contented *part* of Earth; he became her master, justified in wresting from her whatever he needed, without thought for her or his descendants. Dust-bowls were created where once great forests stood. Precious minerals and jewels were mined without regard for anything but profit.

Lately our killing has taken a further step forward. It is now no longer confined to the destruction of forests and oil reserves that can never be replaced. We are actually killing the Earth herself. With our poisonous chemicals and our way of life that requires commodities such as nuclear power, we are polluting the land and the seas. As a result, because that symbiosis still exists whether we like it or not, we are not only becoming increasingly unhealthy, we have even created new diseases as a direct result of pollution.

When we envisage the Earth as a living organism, her whole being vitally affected by what takes place on her surface, a very tricky and complex question poses itself about places all over the world at which mass deaths have occurred. Should the battlefields and concentration camp sites of

70

Western Europe continue to be visited as shrines? Or is there a case for dismantling them and doing all we humanly can to give back life to those sites which are like dead scars on the surface of the Earth?

In the case of the concentration camps there is admittedly a strong argument for keeping these sites intact: no one should forget what happened there; each of us should face the implications of being a member of the human race which allowed such things to happen. The horror and disbelief felt by those who visit the camps, however much they think themselves prepared, confronts them with a view of mankind which is shattering in a way no other sight could be. If all life is interconnected, how much can any of us deny responsibility for these events? How would we have behaved had we been a prisoner there? How much dare we disassociate ourselves from the role of captor/killer? Is our shadow side buried in such shallow ground that, given the right circumstances, it could rise to serve the cause of evil? How is it possible that such events took place, and how can they be prevented from recurring?

That such questions should result from visits to the camps is undoubtedly good, but I would like, with the greatest possible respect for all those who both died and survived the camps, to present an alternative. If they were dismantled and woods planted in their place, these deeply contaminated areas of the Earth would gradually be released from the crippling hold of what happened there. Those deadened spots would no longer be choking the flow of creative love that could constantly be offered to mankind by our planet. Destroying the physical reality of the camps would in *no* way belittle the agony of those who suffered there. Nor would it in any way condemn them to be forgotten. The facts are recorded in a multitude of books and film. Again and again they will emerge to become alive for the next generation. Their imprint is burned deeply into the collective psyche. Their evidence has to be accepted by mankind, constantly strengthening our resolve to prevent their recurrence. The camps would be dismantled for the sake of the Earth herself. The repercussions on mankind would be vastly beneficial. These pockets of hatred would no longer be drawing to themselves new waves of hatred to perpetuate what we most hope to move beyond.

One imagines that the Earth has an inborn capacity to deal, in a very ordered and loving way, with the deaths occurring on every part of her at all times of the day and night. Those that comply with natural rhythms presumably occasion her no pain: a visitor's stay completed, he moves on. She bids him farewell, her own cyclical life unbroken. But at the camp sites, where every spiritual and secular law has been smashed, this convenant between man and the Earth has been violently thrown out of gear. The motives leading to the deaths and the methods of bringing them about have not only seared the Earth's body, they must also have overpowered her by the sheer weight of numbers. What can she do with this burden? How can she disperse it, however great her love? With these grim events that bore no relationship to what she has understood to be her role since the beginning of human life, did she not herself begin to die, as layer upon layer of fear, despair and death were piled onto her?

It is only this inherent strength of the Earth that could have compensated in some measure for the fact that the inmates of the camps perished without the ritual and individual attention of priest or rabbi that they considered essential to their passing. But even she has her limits, and many souls who were not able to release themselves from the horrors of their death are still trapped in the poisoned atmosphere of the camps.

Can we really allow this situation to continue? If members of all the countries involved were to celebrate rituals of forgiveness on each of the sites, so that the ties of hatred be broken and the Earth given a chance to repair her wounds, would this not be a great triumph of love over hatred, giving our planet the opportunity of once again performing her proper role.

A dismantling of the camps could also constitute a giant act of vicarious forgiveness on behalf of all those who died with bitterness and hatred in their hearts. Until this has been done either by them or for them, our nations will be re-populated over and over again by these souls living out that hatred.

7. *The Palace of Immortality on the Happy Isles from Chinese mythology. The three gods of Joyful Existence are crossing the sea, followed by the Royal Mother of the Western Paradise.*

Chapter 19

AIDS

Into the category of diseases which we have ourselves created, fall candida albicans, ME (Myalgic encephalitis) and AIDS, in all of which the immune system is in some way weakened or disrupted. Our unhealthy diet and stress-filled lives, our often indiscriminate use of antibiotics and our polluted air have all contributed to the process. But essentially these are all diseases caused by our killer attitude towards the Earth.

If AIDS becomes part of the global process through which humanity recognizes its abuse of the planet and once more accepts responsibility for the environment, then the acute suffering caused by this illness will not have been in vain. With a change of lifestyle that eliminates long-accumulated stress patterns, re-stabilizes our immune systems and re-connects us with the Earth, the disease can gradually die out.

The aspect of humanity most deeply affected by the dying of the earth is its powers of regeneration. That AIDS should be a sexually-transmitted illness is therefore not coincidental. Are we not being asked to consider carefully the travesty that mankind has made of sexuality: the cruelty and pain engendered by its abuses, the sadness caused by infidelity? What negative effects do people suffer from by engaging in either heterosexual or homosexual prostitution? What does the heartlessness of a marriage of convenience do to someone's spiritual development?

For centuries we have found no satisfactory solutions to any of these questions. We have muddled along. Now AIDS with its death-dealing power is forcing us to find solutions and act on them.

Can the first stage be to develop, on a collective scale, the heart qualities which are such an essential, but often disregarded, element of sexuality? Perhaps one of the roles of this disease is to help us recognize that without them we will never surmount the greed and strife which are plunging us into one calamity after another.

The other issue to which our collective attention is being directed by AIDs is that of re-aligning ourselves with the meaning and possibilities of our creativity, which is such an integral part of sexuality. By so disassociating ourselves from nature, what have we destroyed in ourselves? What source of strength and imagination have we blocked off? Man is potentially an immensely creative creature; some would even say that he could aspire to being a co-creator with God, taking us onwards to ever-new wonders. Instead, by so consistently disregarding his sources of true strength in the Earth and in the Heavens, he has put his creative powers to lamentable use.

This in our modern world is partly due also to another factor: that of feeling such profound impotence that we denigrate our creativity and use it only destructively. Yet the exchange between the individual and the collective *is* two-way. What is happening to one, deeply affects the other. Great swings of fashion in thought, belief and behaviour sweep from time to time through every area of life, leaving only the most dedicated individualists untouched. But the influence of the individual on the collective is equally strong. And this fact we must hold on to as we try to re-assess creativity and the use to which we can put it. In the anonymity of modern life, where so many people are reduced to the status of a number in their apartment block, or in the social security system, this is not easy. Yet that interplay is very real. What one individual can achieve is enormous.

for AIDS sufferers who feel their lives to be without meaning because of their premature curtailment, dying can be very bitter. This sense of being cheated is also often exacerbated by the circumstances surrounding their death: many have been rejected by their closest family and friends; the lack of specialized medical help available makes them very angry; seeing themselves as unjust victims of a social ill, they die in the worst possible frame of mind.

If only this attitude can be reversed, so that the patients see their death as helping to bring about the change of heart mankind so desperately needs. Their emotions could then be channelled into compassion and love rather than bitterness, into prayer or meditation for others instead of hatred on their own behalf.

In a disease of such proportions and significance as AIDS, there must conversely be a great deal that the collective can do for the individual. As society gradually comes to realize that death is a transition and initiation, not an annihilation, a new understanding will give courage to all those who are dying.

Chapter 20

The Rise and Fall of Civilizations

In the larger cycles of death represented by the rise and fall of civilizations, each successive one, ever since Cro-Magnon replaced Neanderthal man, has hastened the completion of the former cycle by destroying as much as possible of its culture as well as annihilating its inhabitants. Instead of retaining the positive aspects of the older culture, fear so dominates this process that the slate has each time to be wiped clean at whatever cost.

When Akhnaton's brave attempt at establishing a mono-theistic religion in Ancient Egypt failed, his enemies razed to the ground all trace of his existence. It is only the devoted work of modern archaeologists that is slowly reclaiming that evidence from the desert. When the Spaniards went to South America as Conquistadores thinking only of gold, they were so blind to the very advanced architecture, social structures and religions of the Incas, Mayans and Aztecs that they were able to destroy them without compunction; only sick and weak remnants of their civilizations carried on. When the Romans conquered Europe, they killed off most of the Celts, destroying untold religious and artistic riches. This tradition has continued with the near-extinction of the Bushmen by the settlers of South Africa, the Maori by the New Zealanders and the North American Indians by the Americans.

Only recently have we begun to realize what tragic losses mankind has sustained through this carnage. With painstaking care the beliefs and traditions of the shattered peoples are now being pieced together, but unless the essence of the old beliefs can be carried forward to become a living and creative part of modern life, they will remain as anthropological phenomena, of use only to historians.

This cyclical destruction of progressive civilizations has meant, in a sense, that we have had repeatedly to start from scratch instead of building on acquired knowledge. But why do we feel so threatened by earlier thoughts and beliefs? Why should we need a totally empty surface on which to establish a new way of being? It seems very illogical and wasteful. Especially as we see that on the rare occasions when an incoming civilization had the courage to absorb into itself some of the holy sites and culture of the outgoing people, great strength was derived from the process.

So strongly is this pattern engrained in humanity that we find the same behaviour occurring in individual lives. When a new relationship is formed, for instance, the history of former lovers or spouses has to be more or less expunged in order to allay the jealousies or insecurities of the new partner. Although curiosity may lead him or her to question the past, the answers given will deliberately create the impression, (even if a false one,) that the new relationship is so satisfactory that it obliterates memories of the old one. Even in the animal world, this same pattern is present. If an already-pregnant lioness is taken over by another lion, he will kill her cubs at birth.

Yet there is such richness in the past. Is it not time that we began to encompass mankind's total history into our thinking. By claiming our roots in the far-distant past, we can abolish these arid deaths of past civilizations. What is carried forward by future generations has not died. In order to start this process for the collective, we can begin by acknowledging and integrating all our past lives into our Now, acknowledging that they have shaped us in the same way that one civilization shapes the next. We are as we are because of them, and the continuity of our personal soul thread, like that of mankind's collective soul thread, makes a nothingness of death.

Chapter 21

Voodoo and Curses

Voodoo or deaths caused by the use of magic and suggestion are subjects beyond the scope of this book, yet they need a brief mention because they are and have been such an important part of life in many areas of the world. Although very foreign to the civilized mind, their mysterious workings exert a total hold on those who are brought up within their sphere of influence.

It is through the use of a 'witness', such as a nail paring or tuft of hair from the intended victim, that contact is established by the voodoo practitioner. Having incorporated this witness into a likeness of the victim, he is then able to bring about his death. In Haiti, Jamaica, or other places where black magic is commonly practiced, knowledge that a curse has been placed on you by the voodoo doctor is enough to remove all resistance to death. Distance, however great, constitutes no barrier to the effectiveness of a curse. There are a number of deaths recorded in London hospitals of people who have been admitted as the target of a spell. Although bearing no visible symptoms that could cause death, they have simply turned to the wall and died.

A phenomenon more familiar in Europe, yet very closely linked to the above, is that of the curses put on a house or family. Of these, the most common one connected with houses precludes any son surviving long enough to inherit. A tragic instance of this concerned a family who lived in a beautiful old house on the Sussex downs. When the Second World War started, the father and his two older sons were immediately called up. The eldest was killed within months. A year later the second one was torpedoed in the Atlantic. When next home on leave, the father entered into frantic discussion with his solicitor and several other people crucially involved in the complicated legal and financial ensnarlments surrounding the house. Their efforts were in vain. The family could not sell. For them to move out while still owning the house would not free them from the curse. The time came for the next two sons to enlist. Within a year both of them were dead; so was their father. The youngest son was not of an age to fight in the war, but he died shortly afterwards of cancer.

Another famous curse began in Egypt in the 1930s when an English tourist mocked the most sacred moment of a temple ritual. The priest in charge then publicly declared a curse on the man and his family. His words were greeted by laughter. But the reality of the priest's powers quickly asserted themselves. The Englishman's wife, who flew back to England a few days before him, was killed in a mid-air explosion. Her spectacular death was followed by a series of such wildly improbable 'accidents' involving his close family, that no one could any longer ridicule the curse. A renowned Egyptologist was despatched to the temple to beg that it be removed as quickly as possible. But this, he was told, could not be done. It had been imposed by three priests and could only be removed by those same three men. One of them had since died. As the years passed, the disasters which had dogged the family became rarer, and finally died out.

In the same way that deaths can be intentionally willed by voodoo practitioners, so too can people will themselves to die. This happens almost exclusively in 'primitive' societies, where people are more in tune with their bodies and the cycles of nature. When they have become too ill or old to be of use to the tribe, Eskimoes, North American Indians and members of several other cultures simply lie down and die.

Chapter 22

The Death of Animals

The question of whether or not animals survive death, and in what conditions, is a subject on which teachings vary considerably. So do those about their possible reincarnation. Whether animals evolve within the animal kingdom, or can even progress into the human world are also questions to which a variety of answers are given.

For animals, death is a less traumatic event than for humans. Far more instinctively aware of their life cycle than we are, they accept death as it occurs rather than anticipating it with dread. Bearing this in mind – and provided of course that no pain or fear are introduced – it is essential that pets and farm animals never live on beyond what is comfortable for them. When suffering has become a major element in their life, they should be allowed or even helped to die, however great their owner's grief.

Where pain and fear do co-exist with death, other considerations have to be taken into account. The first of these is the anguish which will be carried over into that animal's group soul. And here the expression 'group soul' has to be differentiated from that term applied to humans. Amongst animals there is no individuation – especially in the lower species. They therefore share a group soul, rather than having an individual soul which is linked to the others in its group. Because of this, the impact of an animal's experience on his group is even more direct and intense than that of a human who, although contributing at death his entire life experience to his soul group, first filters it through his own soul evolution. So the shock felt by a pheasant that has been shot or a pig that has had its throat slit registers with anguish on the entire pheasant or pig soul. It would not seem too fanciful to imagine that amongst species whose deaths are now predominantly violent, a reluctance to incarnate must be growing. This in turn must be causing a very uncomfortable situation within the animal kingdom. Earth was intended as a place where each species could develop in its own particular way. For virtually the entire plant and animal kingdoms, man has unsettled that plan. The consequences of this are very worrying.

All sudden and painful deaths which cut short an animal's natural life cycle must be affecting the atmosphere in the same way that we saw happening around battlefields. A pig being taken to the slaughterhouse will start screaming with fear long before any sight or sound could possibly warn it of its fate. To the eye of a 'sensitive', death and fear have both shape and colour. Our present large-scale killing for sport and food production is crowding our planet's etheric body with highly undesirable shapes and colours.

The other human manipulation of animals which is creating untold shame and guilt for mankind is animal experimentation. It divides into two types: experiments made in the name of medicine and those carried out in order to test consumer products.

Leaving aside for the moment all moral considerations, there exists in the first case a fundamentally false assumption. Only the immense financial interests of the laboratories and drug companies could maintain the untenable proposition that animals can substitute for humans as testing grounds for the effect of a drug. The contrary has been demonstrated many many times. Drugs which had proven successful in curing animals of laboratory-induced conditions turned out to be not only unhelpful, but at times rankly dangerous to humans. The history of Thalidomide and its catastrophic effect on those whose mothers had taken the drug while pregnant, is a dramatic instance amongst many less-publicized ones. All these drugs claimed to be 'fully tested' on animals. Man has a far more complex physical body than even the most evolved animal. In addition, unlike animals, man has six subtle bodies. A guinea pig or monkey is therefore a creature so different to man that the suffering to which these laboratory animals are condemned is often without value. Only an untruthful propaganda feeding on people's fears perpetuates this infamous system.

In the testing of marketable products, the justification for killing millions of animals every year is even weaker. Everyone *knows*, and has done for decades, that cigarette smoke is harmful to the lungs. Experiments to prove this help no one. Why then should hundreds of thousands of dogs spend their entire lives motionless in cages, with cigarette smoke being forced down their throats so that they die in agony, their lungs lacerated by nicotine wounds? Only the most corrupt and senseless system of government grants providing safe livings for laboratories and the breeders of the doomed animals can explain this nonsensical behaviour. Nothing can justify it. If the facts were more widely known, surely the public would force the government to abolish these despicable practices. The adverse karma being built up between us and the animal kingdoms does not bear thinking about.

Only the gravest misconception concerning the consciousness of animals and the relationship that should exist between them and man could have created the deeply disturbing situation which has existed throughout almost all human history. Very close and beautiful relationships do of course develop between individuals and their animals. The love and affinity that can grow between an elephant and his mahout, a horse and his jockey, or a sheepdog and his shepherd are legendary. But they are, alas, exceptions. Use them, eat them, and don't worry too much about their life conditions, has been our common attitude. Man's supposed 'superiority' to the animals has been the derisory vindication for such behaviour.

It is through an understanding of the animal kingdom, each species of which makes a different and invaluable contribution to the whole, that man can best maintain contact with that part of himself which needs to evolve alongside his intellect., If the latter is allowed to take over completely, the instinctual part of him will die – with disastrous results. Our present ecological situation is an excellent example of this process.

So much of man's shadow material has been spilled onto the animals throughout the ages that instead of being able to teach us by example their wonderfully creative relationship to nature, they have in some disastrous way been disempowered. Our rejection of their proffered gift has also deprived their collective deaths of that energy of rebirth which would exist had their lives been truly fulfilled; their potential contribution to their group soul is thereby impoverished. And here lies the great responsibility of all human beings towards all animals: the more we make their experience of earth positive, the more they will raise the consciousness of the animal world. A few happy exchanges of love and service recorded by a handful of pets is not enough. Those billions of animals who have been hunted and used throughout history have fed panic and disarray into their group's consciousness. Until we offer them something better, it is with the sum of all this negative experience that they will keep returning to Earth.

Although death may be less conscious and dramatic for animals than for humans, the form it takes for them is nevertheless very important to Earth's total scheme. The death of an elephant trapped and shot by poachers for its ivory, or that of a badger choking to death in its set for 'sport', are not only cruel and useless, they rob the animal's life of all meaning. So too does the lethal combination of our ruthlessly efficient abattoires and our bulging dustbins of uneaten food.

Where a death follows the course of nature there is already meaning in it, so that however sad we may find the sight of a beautiful gazelle being killed by a lion, the fact that its flesh will feed the lion cubs fulfills the gazelle's life. The message it takes back to its group soul will not be a shattered one.

In contrast to some Eastern beliefs, Western esoteric teaching states categorically that transmigration moves in only one direction: very slowly the animals are working their way up the evolutionary scale. Humans, whatever their behaviour, cannot 'revert' to being an animal of any kind.

There is less agreement amongst occultists and psychics as to the exact conditions provided for animals after death. One of the main disputes arises over whether or not they share with humans the same regions of the higher worlds. It seems unlikely in view of the fact that people and animals are capable of receiving such different teachings.

Another debate centres around the question of whether a major step forward is now taking place, allowing certain evolved animals to individuate within their group souls and to eventually incarnate as human beings. If this is so, it is important not to assume that an animal's first life as a man would necessarily be a base or even basic one. The qualities of love and service, loyalty and sensitivity may already have been very well developed in an evolved animal. These characteristics would be carried forward into his human life.

Assuming for the moment that this is now one of the quantum leaps possible, the quality of an individual animal's life becomes even more important. From now on it will not only enhance or detract from the evolution of all dogs, whales, horses etc, it will also directly affect its own progress towards becoming a new human soul.

In all the animal mysteries and traditions, each animal family represents particular qualities which are also to be found in human beings. Cats, for instance, have always been connected with healing: the witches' familiar was usually feline, and in ancient Egypt the temples of the cat Goddess Bakst were centres of healing. Horses, on the other hand, have always been associated with power and control, whether they were part of a chariot race, a cavalry charge, or a ritualized hunt. Dolphins and whales have in all cultures been closely linked to the areas of communication, balance and integrity. The fact that we have chosen to treat these highly intelligent creatures with such fierce cruelty that their very existence is now endangered, makes one wonder at the

8. *Dante's Heaven of the Fixed Stars is the ninth of the concentric heavenly realms through which the soul passes in his spiritual journey. (Gustave Dore's engraving for* The Divine Comedy*).*

courage they must need to keep sending to Earth yet more members of a soul group so weighed down with sadness. What love for mankind they show in trying over and over again to help us understand the necessity and joy of true communication with the animal kingdoms.

Appendices

Ritual for Forgiveness

Having spoken of forgiveness as being such an important part of dying, I would like to suggest a ritual to help in the on-going process of forgiving and being forgiven. In either case the form of the ritual is the same.

This ceremony is designed in such a way that it can be done alone, or with the person directly concerned, or in a group. The latter can be very powerful indeed if there is harmony amongst its members and if the person seeking forgiveness feels completely uninhibited by their presence. The form of the ritual is so simple that even if someone were already confined to bed, it could still be performed.

Start by marking out two circles on the floor with pieces of string, small pebbles, candles, or anything else you feel to be appropriate. The circles should not touch each other. Symbolically this represents the safety which each person can feel within his circle; it also symbolizes the total choice each separate entity has about the extent of his contact with the other person.

In the centre of each circle place a chair or a cushion, whichever you prefer, but the two should be of the same height. Beside both chairs or cushions place a selection of coloured crepe paper, already cut into strips about three inches wide and three foot long.

Ensure that you will be undisturbed during the ritual by unplugging the telephone, putting a note on the door, etc.

If you like candles as part of a ceremony, place one in each corner of the room, dedicating them to peace and protection.

They should be lit just before entering your circle.

If the other person concerned cannot be there, give reality to his presence by placing his photograph or some symbolic object on his chair.

If the ceremony is being enacted by a group, assign to each of them whatever role needs filling: that of impartial onlooker, an emotion or event that needs forgiveness, the sound or colour of your feelings, etc. Instruct them as to how active or passive you would like them to be.

If there is nothing you would like to add to the above, take your places in the circles, facing each other. If a group is performing the ritual, its members should form a large circle around the two small ones. During the next few minutes of silence, invoke the aid of your Higher Self, your guide, your power animal, your guardian angel, or whatever assistance you most rely on.

Now start explaining to the person you want to forgive or be forgiven by, the reasons for which you think this release necessary. As you talk, facts and feelings of whose existence you have been unaware, may emerge. Allow them the space to become a living part of your story.

When you have finished, hand over to the other person. If he is unable to be there, or his presence would have been unbearable to you, move into his circle and from *his* point of view and from *his* space, speak on his behalf. This may at first seem insuperably difficult, but this exercise in objectivity and impartiality may well prove to be a major element in your catharsis.

When statements have been made from both circles, take your strips of crepe paper and chose a suitable colour to represent each of the events and feelings of which you have spoken. For an angry memory you could, for instance, select a scarlet strip and for feelings of envy a yellowy-green one. Be guided by your intuition rather than by any classic colour interpretation. This is *your* story and *your* personality.

When all the ingredients have been named out loud and assembled, start plaiting them together, consciously noting how intimately each emotion and happening affects all the others, and how significantly the entire pattern will be altered by the forgiveness of even one strand. If yours is a very intricate design built up over many hundreds of years, the ritual should ideally be performed several times. But if this is your last opportunity in this incarnation to release the maximum number of strands you can manage, simply trust. As much as possible will be done; further time and help will be given to you between incarnations now that you have shown yourself willing to deal with this karma.

Once the two plaits are complete, place them on the ground touching both circles, symbolizing the effect these feelings and events have had on *both* your lives. After a few minutes of silence, concentrating on what it will really mean for you to have exteriorized this hatred and despair, take back your plait and begin to unweave it, consciously releasing each strand as it falls to the floor. Then give time to the other person to do the same.

When you have blown out the candles and dismantled the circles, dispose of the crepe paper in some definitive way – either by burning or shredding the strips. When returning the cushions, or any other props you may have used to their original places, be sure to de-role them. They have taken on powerful projections during the past hour. Finish the ritual by giving thanks to all those who have helped you, even if you have not been consciously aware of them.

Ritual for an Aborted Child and its Mother

Whatever the circumstances which created the necessity for a woman to have an abortion, she rarely emerges from it unscathed. Even if her first reaction is relief at having safely terminated the pregnancy, she is almost inevitably left with feelings that are very hard to assimilate, especially if she has had to go through the experience alone, as is so often the case. These feelings will probably include either intense loneliness, resentment, anger at being abandoned, fear of discovery, or great sadness at not being able to have the child. All of these will have been intensified by the anxiety and physical fear associated with the operation itself.

However commonplace, even to some extent accepted, abortion may have become, it is an operation like no other, evoking a deep sense of loss and dismay registered at a level she may not even have known existed. If this sense of loss, mingled with other negative reactions, is compounded by a sense of guilt, the results can be catastrophic, influencing her life, whether consciously or not, for many years.

In addition to the psychological trauma briefly mentioned above, there will also be strong physiological factors involved. 'The body remembers' is a saying which carries much truth. The body in this case will have been imprinted by two very distressing memories. First of all the shock of having a new cycle abruptly terminated, however summarily it had been acknowledged. And secondly, the memory of the operation's attack on its most intimate feminine self. The latter cannot help influencing to some degree, again possibly unconsciously, the body's future sexual relationships. If she is fortunate, the woman will at some time receive the tenderness which can heal these scars. If not, the help of a therapist could usefully be sought.

The fact that no ceremony or ritual exists in honour of an aborted child is perhaps one of the foremost reasons why this event often continues to retain such a prominent position in a woman's psyche. Most other occurrences of similar magnitude have some form of ritual which helps exteriorize and categorize people's feelings.

For those who have undergone an abortion, recently or long ago, the following ritual is offered as a possible help towards healing. It can be done either in silence or accompanied by music or words. Its symbolism can be acted out or not.

The first part of the ritual is concerned with the child, who has not received the loving care it would have known had it reached full term. Start then by taking in your imagination a beautiful new-born baby to some quiet, well-loved place in the country and ask that the Earth help you give this child the nourishment and love you were prevented from giving.

When you feel ready, lay the baby on a bed of softly coloured flowers. Surround it with sunshine, your favourite trees, the sound of birds, everything you most love about the country. Then imagine a cord of plaited pink and green ribbons linking the child to the very centre of the Earth, from where heart energy and love and warmth will feed it.

Its existence as a beloved soul will now be acknowledged in a way denied to it by the circumstances surrounding its entry into the world. To name the baby at this point could be very helpful. It would add to your sense of its real and separate identity. If you can find no name which feels right, you could identify it by a quality: Tenderness or Serenity, or whatever you would wish for your child.

When your feelings of love for the baby have been expressed, release it – fully and joyfully – perhaps with an upward gesture of the arms. Sounding aloud whatever note is in your heart would be a good way to round off this part of the ritual.

Once the child has been released, turn to your own needs. An essential start is that you forgive yourself, whatever the circumstances and reasons for the abortion. Just sit quietly and allow compassion to flow over you. If it is helpful, cry – not for the baby, but for yourself. When you again feel really calm, move on to the next stage.

Try to identify individually each of the heavy, soiled, unhappy or messy feelings that you may associate with the operation or anyone involved in it. Really look at them. Given them a shape, or a colour, or whatever most effectively objectivizes the feeling for you. Then take them one by one and consign them to either a fire or some body of water, whichever seems to you most purifying and final. These are feelings of which you want now to be forever free. Walking in a stream or washing your hands and face could complete this process.

The third step in the ritual seeks to connect you deeply with the Earth. This is as important for the mother as it was for the child. Because it is through the three lower chakras that we know and absorb Earth energies, and it is these chakras which have been most assaulted by the abortion, they will need the healing that only the Earth can give.

Chose again in your imagination some well-loved place in the country and lie flat on the earth. Breathing very deeply and rhythmically, ask to be made whole. If you feel that it would stabilize and help you, imagine a cord attaching you to the centre of the earth where an abundance of warmth and love can feed you. Use for your cord the colours of the earth and of summer corn fields entwined with green, so that all the strength and dependability of nature is available to you. If you feel a need for the colour red to revivify and revitalize you, interweave that colour amongst the others.

Sound has a very deep healing quality. You might find that sounding the note of your pain could bring a final release. Don't be shy. Identify the most difficult moment of your pregnancy; look at it fully and without fear; then allow to rise from your deepest womanhood whatever sound demands to come forth.

If you feel that this ritual could cause you grief beyond what you could bear on your own, ask a friend to go through it with you. Also remember that the above is a suggestion only; as long as the main intentions are retained, all details can be altered.

Ritual for the Father of an Aborted Child

Social mores have until recently allowed the majority of men to forego most feelings of guilt and responsibility over an abortion. If they behaved honorably from a financial point of view, they were on the whole thought to have done their duty. Except in cases of very deep love, or where particularly sensitive men were involved, they were able to disregard the emotional aspects of the event. Because the pregnancy had little physical reality, it lacked in a way all reality. For many it could be regarded as merely a nuisance or a lamentable failure of the 'precautions' taken. For them a positive pregnancy test could easily be disassociated from the concept of a real child. Their main concern tended to be for a clean and safe operation.

But where love and responsibility exist, the situation is entirely different, and can be quite as painful for the father as the mother, because whatever the circumstances creating the need for an abortion, the father will almost certainly have been aware of them before the pregnancy occurred – except, of course, in one of the rarer cases when an abortion is performed on medical grounds. His feelings of guilt will then encompass not only the child who has been irresponsibly created, but also the mother whom he has placed in a highly disagreeable and potentially dangerous situation.

The more general reasons for the change in attitude which many men are now experiencing are complex. The Women's Movement has certainly incited women to refuse to be 'left holding the baby'. And the Courts are now more ready to uphold women's rights. But there are also deeper factors at work. In the same way that women are exploring their masculine selves, so are men starting to discover their feminine. Empathizing into what was until recently considered to be exclusively feminine territory, is now admissible. Men can allow themselves to express regret; they needn't hide the tenderness they feel for a child conceived out of love. They can admit to their real distress at having exposed a woman to the ordeal of an abortion. This violation to her body can become a vivid part of their own vicarious experience.

So strong is the effect of these new psychological trends, that they appear to be working retrospectively. Many of the men expressing the need for a ritual such as this one are older men for whom the re-emergence of this memory is so disturbing that they are willing to re-live it in order to make peace with it.

For these men a ritual to deal with the emotional, psychological and moral issues raised by an abortion is as needed as it is for women. The one proposed here, like that for a mother, is first for the child and secondly for the father. The first part being the same as in the earlier ritual, (see p 000), it has not been repeated here.

The second part starts with a request for self-forgiveness. This is vitally important. Feeling guilty about what has happened can help no one. If you can affirm *aloud* that this forgiveness has been granted you, it will be invested with added power.

Next ask the baby to forgive you for having given it the pain of descending to earth, and for then not having protected its life. During a quiet meditation, try to understand the reason for that soul's short visit to earth. Was it primarily for itself? Or have one or both of its parents been given a gift of which they should be aware? By discovering the answers to these questions, you may well validate the baby's life. The Law of Economy is strictly adhered to in the spiritual world, and it is highly unlikely that this pregnancy was not significant for the three souls concerned.

The next part of the ritual involves calling upon your

ancestors – and, if so desired, those of the woman involved. This unfulfilled pregnancy may well have been intended in part to awaken your personal sense of continuity and family. Your ancestors' input can do much to make you understand the event from a wider perspective. Sit quietly for a few minutes, making yourself receptive to anything they wish to convey to you, remembering that they knew beforehand that this child would never continue the family line. Realizing this fact may well dissolve many of your regrets.

It is now the turn of your own emotions. Allow to the fore all that you have not yet expressed. If there has been disagreement about the abortion, really feel your fury at the woman who insisted on aborting your child. Vent your resentment on whatever circumstances prevented the baby's birth. If long-suppressed tears are ready to flow, cry. And if neither anger nor tears seem needed, just sit quietly mourning and absorbing the baby, yet disentangling yourself from it so that both of you can be fully released.

The final section of the ritual could, if wanted, consist of a quiet statement to the mother, of all your emotions and doubts, however passionate or negative. In the setting of a ritual, this could be very releasing without causing further enmeshment between you and her.

The New Age Funeral
by Sir George Trevelyan

I write about funerals in our remarkable time when a new vision for humankind is being born. Is this a mournful subject? For whom do we mourn? Is it for the soul that has been released back into the Light? Or is it for ourselves in our sense of loss?

We must learn to apply the spiritual world-view in our living and in our dying. Hold to the concept that the 'I AM' in each of us is a spiritual entity, a droplet of God, housed for a period in the beautifully designed temple of the body. This body is of course perishable and can die and be destroyed. But this only releases the immortal droplet to rise again into the spiritual plane from which it descended at birth.

God is Life. Life is God. Life cannot die. The notion is absurd! The sheath in which the soul sojourns for a while on the Earth plane will of course, once the life within it has withdrawn, break down and revert again to humus. This is what begins to happen as soon as the soul withdraws at so-called death. The body disintegrates but the entity, the droplet, is immortal and it is absurd to think that the divine being, a strand of the Living God, can 'die' with the body.

Yet by ancient tradition and convention we still act as if this is what happens. We lay the coffin in the earth and say that he or she now sleeps or is resting – to eternity. It is customary thinking offered in respect for the 'dead'.

But the I AM is a deathless being. A soul and spirit, vibrantly alive since it is a strand of the ocean of God-Life, is tacitly assumed now to rest and sleep in the churchyard, under the sod! It is somehow felt that reverence and respect for the one that has passed on calls for this concept.

Surely we need to change this picture in a New Age Funeral. The truth is affirmed in the old hymn:

> "Dust thou art, to dust returning,
> Was not spoken of the soul!"

In no way is it disrespectful to the 'dead' or unsympathetic to the bereaved to declare that the spiritual entity remains very much alive. More alive indeed, since embodiment means that the spirit takes on the weight of matter and plunges into the darker, heavier conditions offered by the earth plane.

And for a purpose. Earth is a training school for souls. Earth is the planet of freedom. We are here that we may learn ultimately to come back to God as a co-creator, in freedom. It is a majestic picture. This wonderful planet was chosen as the setting for the great experiment – that the Tenth Hierarchy, "a little lower than the angels, but crowned with glory and honour", should here learn to handle freedom and come back to the Father of free choice, having overcome the lower desires and temptations of the sense world. This planet thus is evolving something new in the universe: a being consciously directing and controlling itself, its emotions and its reactions, so that it may be worthy to become, (to repeat the phrase) a co-creator with God.

This ultimate achievement takes an immense length of time and therefore many incarnations, as we flounder through temptations, desires and disastrous blunders. But the goal is that we wake up and of free choice say "I will go back to the Father". We see a prospect far more rewarding than merely satisfying desire.

> "Is not the whole of Eternity mine?"

That statement is the closing affirmation in an essay on "The Education of the Human Race" by the German philosopher Lessing in the late 18th century, the first European presentation of the case for re-incarnation.

Now, what should this thinking do to the conduct of our funerals? Recently I was asked to give the address at the funeral of a great friend of mine, David Ballantyne, a craftsman of truly Renaissance proportions, who could turn his hand to any craft or art in solving the challenges and problems of creation. As I stood beside the coffin before a hundred mourners I sympathised with the bereaved family, praised and assessed the remarkable life achievement of this creative spirit and then affirmed my conviction that He, the spiritual being, was *not* in the coffin and by no means could we or would we 'lay him to rest' in the churchyard! David was now a free spirit released from the limitations of embodiment. We were mourning not for him, but for the loss we felt. And, since it is clear that on the eternal and timeless 'higher plane' the spirit will be drawn instantly to the souls to which it is linked in love and thought, it was logically certain that 'David' was assuredly with us, drawn by the love of those who had gathered in his honour. Wonderful thought! So I made bold to speak directly to him! "David, great soul, beloved friend, go forward. Be released from embodiment. Carry your creativity into wider and eternal fields. We send you forth to your release with joy. *You*, we know, are very much alive, indeed more alive since you have shed the heavy body. Not farewell – fare forward, Traveller!"

Will not this attitude and viewpoint call for a New Age Funeral of a new type? All sympathy to the family and friends who have lost the presence of the loved one; all honour and loving support for the soul in its exploration into higher worlds. And that soul is so near, for when we think to him or her with love it will, on the subtler level, be instantly with us.

So at the emotional moment of bodily separation, let there be grand music as we release our friend from earthly limitation to go forward into the Light.

New Age thinking calls for a re-casting of the funeral service, which will lose nothing of its dignity, but will approach closer to the great truth that the human soul comes again and again into earth embodiment until it has cleansed and purged itself of egoism and can truly come back to God as a co-creator. As souls progress in their long training and evolution in the school of Earth, death will increasingly be experienced as RELEASE INTO LIGHT.

Then the *Ceremony of Dying* will take on new joy, beauty and dignity as a bridging point between two worlds, which truly interpenetrate when love and sympathy are consciously maintained.

Recommended Reading List

Beard, Paul: *Living On: A Study of Altered Consciousness after Death*, Pilgrim, 1987.

Greaves, Helen: *Testimony of Light*, Spearman, 1969.

Grey, Margot: *Return from Death: An Exploration of the Near-death Experience*, Arkana, 1985.

Levine, Stephen: *Who Dies? An Investigation of Conscious Living and Conscious Dying*, Gateway, 1988.

Lorimer, David: *Survival?*, Routledge, 1984.

Lorimer, David *Whole in One: The Near Death Experience and the Ethic of Connectedness*, Arkana, 1991.

McCall, Kenneth: *Healing the Family Tree*.

Moody, Raymond: *Life After Life*, Bantam, 1983.

Swain, Jasper: *On the Death of my Son*, Turnstone (Thorsons), 1974.

Tudor Pole, Wellesley: *Private Dowding*, Pilgrim, 1917.

Whitton, Joel & Fisher, Joe: *Life Between Life: Scientific Explorations into the Void Separating one Incarnation with Another*, Grafton, 1986.

Visions of Hope

A video of
The Near Death Experience

On 8th August 1949, Church Army Captain Edmund Wilbourne was certified dead from pleurisy following a severe illness, and the final funeral arrangements were put in hand. Two hours later he awoke in the mortuary of Crumpsall Hospital having undergone a most extraordinary visionary experience which was to transform his life and remove all fear of death.

Captain Wilbourne's experience is not unique, but one of several thousand well attested cases of people who have returned from clinical death with a clear memory of their continued existence outside the physical body.

This film, interposed with professional comments from doctors and theologians is a documentary account of six individuals who have had a 'near death experience' and its powerful effect on their lives. The discovery of these experiences will perhaps be regarded in time to come as the most important single contribution in shaping our attitudes to life and death.

'*Once you have been in this light, and experienced its peace and love . . . it changes all your values and you still know that death does not really exist.*' Elizabeth Kubler Ross, MD.

'*We are seeing the first few moments of life after death.*' The Ven Michael Perry.

'*I know without a doubt that I am not my body.*' Trudy Iles.

'*It's given me a sense of loving the Earth, but knowing that this is not the final part of the story of me or anyone else.*' Geoff Freed.

'*It brings death out of the closet . . . a message of hope, real hope.*' Joyce Strom Paiken (psychiatric nurse).

This 40 minute video can be ordered from   Greensleeves,
23 All Saints Villas Road,
Cheltenham, Glos. GL52 2HB

at a cost of £18, inc. p & p.